How to Use This Book

Look for these special features in this book:

SIDEBARS, **CHARTS**, **GRAPHS**, and original **MAPS** expand your understanding of what's being discussed—and also make useful sources for classroom reports.

FAQs answer common **F**requently **A**sked **Q**uestions about people, places, and things.

WOW FACTORS offer "Who knew?" facts to keep you thinking.

TRAVEL GUIDE gives you tips on exploring the state—either in person or right from your chair!

PROJECT ROOM provides fun ideas for school assignments and incredible research projects. Plus, there's a guide to primary sources—what they are and how to cite them.

Please note: All statistics are as up-to-date as possible at the time of publication.

Consultants: Geoffrey Cook, Department of Geosciences, University of Rhode Island; Evelyn Sterne, Department of History, University of Rhode Island; William Loren Katz

Book production by The Design Lab

Library of Congress Cataloging-in-Publication Data
Burgan, Michael.
 Rhode Island / by Michael Burgan.
     p. cm.—(America the beautiful. Third series)
 Includes bibliographical references and index.
 ISBN-13: 978-0-531-18590-2
 ISBN-10: 0-531-18590-7
 1. Rhode Island—Juvenile literature. I. Title.
 F79.3.B87 2009
 974.5—dc22   2007037178

Rhode Island

BY MICHAEL BURGAN

Third Series

Children's Press®
An Imprint of Scholastic Inc.
New York ★ Toronto ★ London ★ Auckland ★ Sydney
Mexico City ★ New Delhi ★ Hong Kong
Danbury, Connecticut

CONTENTS

GROWTH AND CHANGE

4

Rhode Island is the birthplace of the American Industrial Revolution. Workers and immigrants struggle to gain their political rights. **48**

MORE MODERN TIMES

5

Rhode Islanders survive the Great Depression and eagerly do their part in World War II. After the war, workers move to the suburbs, factories move out of state, and new industries move in. . . **62**

Explore Rhode Island's spectacular shoreline, rich history, and fun-filled towns. **104**

9

TRAVEL GUIDE

PROJECT ROOM

★

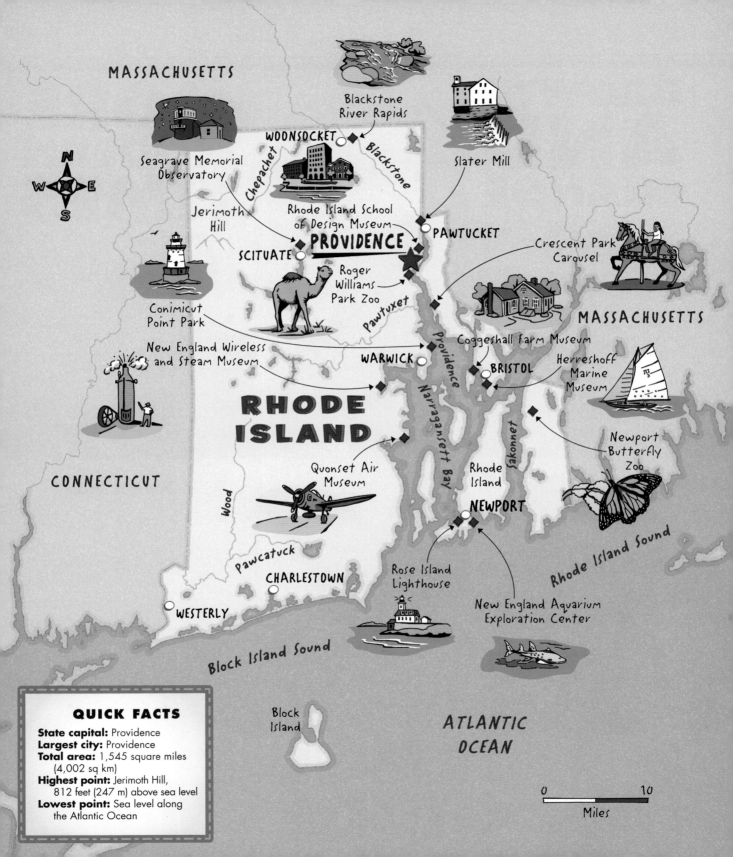

MASSACHUSETTS

Blackstone River Rapids

Slater Mill

Seagrave Memorial Observatory

WOONSOCKET

Chepachet

Blackstone

Jerimoth Hill

Rhode Island School of Design Museum

PROVIDENCE

PAWTUCKET

Crescent Park Carousel

SCITUATE

Roger Williams Park Zoo

MASSACHUSETTS

Conimicut Point Park

Pawtuxet

Coggeshall Farm Museum

New England Wireless and Steam Museum

Providence

BRISTOL

Herreshoff Marine Museum

WARWICK

RHODE ISLAND

Narragansett Bay

Sakonnet

Newport Butterfly Zoo

CONNECTICUT

Quonset Air Museum

Rhode Island

NEWPORT

Rhode Island Sound

Wood

Pawcatuck

CHARLESTOWN

Rose Island Lighthouse

New England Aquarium Exploration Center

WESTERLY

Block Island Sound

ATLANTIC OCEAN

Block Island

QUICK FACTS

State capital: Providence
Largest city: Providence
Total area: 1,545 square miles (4,002 sq km)
Highest point: Jerimoth Hill, 812 feet (247 m) above sea level
Lowest point: Sea level along the Atlantic Ocean

0   10
Miles

Welcome to Rhode Island!

HOW DID RHODE ISLAND GET ITS NAME?

In 1524, Italian explorer Giovanni da Verrazzano spotted a triangle-shaped island in the Atlantic Ocean, about 10 miles (16 kilometers) from the mainland. He thought the small spot of land looked like Rhodes, an island that is part of Greece. Just over a century later, English colonists came to the region Verrazzano had explored. They called their new home Rhode Island, thinking it was the island Verrazzano had seen. Their settlement and others near the town of Providence soon merged to form a colony. When the colony became a state, its official name changed to the State of Rhode Island and Providence Plantations—a long name for the smallest state in the nation!

READ ABOUT

A view of Castle
Hill Lighthouse
in Newport

CHAPTER ONE

LAND

★

O NE OF RHODE ISLAND'S NICK-NAMES IS THE OCEAN STATE, AND WITH GOOD REASON. From Rhode Island's highest point on Jerimoth Hill, 812 feet (247 meters), to its lowest point at sea level, the Atlantic Ocean is never more than a half-hour drive away.

Rhode Island covers just 1,545 square miles (4,002 square kilometers), making it the smallest of the 50 U.S. states. This explains another of its nicknames—Little Rhody.

WORD TO KNOW

glaciers *slow-moving masses of ice*

CARVING THE LAND

The movement of huge sheets of ice called **glaciers** helped form Rhode Island's rivers and rocky shores. Ice several thousand feet thick covered the region that is now Rhode Island at least two different times. The moving ice ground down hills and carved out the river valleys and coastline. As the ice melted, some of the water was trapped in low spots, forming lakes. The last glacier left Rhode Island about 15,000 years ago.

LAND REGIONS

Rhode Island is one of the six states that form New England. It borders two states: Connecticut to the west and Massachusetts to the north and east. The southern part of Rhode Island lies along the Atlantic Ocean.

Rhode Island Geo-Facts

Along with the state's geographical highlights, this chart ranks Rhode Island's land, water, and total area compared to all other states.

Total area; rank . . . . 1,545 square miles (4,002 sq km); 50th
Land; rank . . . . 1,045 square miles (2,707 sq km); 50th
Water; rank . . . . .500 square miles (1,295 sq km); 41st
Inland water; rank . . . . . . 178 square miles (461 sq km); 46th
Coastal water; rank . . . . 9 square miles (23 sq km); 20th
Territorial water; rank . . .314 square miles (813 sq km); 17th
Geographic center . . . Kent, 1 mile (1.6 km) southwest of Crompton
Latitude . . . . 41°09' N to 42°01' N
Longitude . . . . 71°07' W to 71°53' W
Highest point . . . . . . Jerimoth Hill, 812 feet (247 m) above sea level
Lowest point . . . . Sea level along the Atlantic Ocean
Largest city . . . . .Providence
Longest river . . . . Blackstone

Source: U.S. Census Bureau; U.S. Geological Survey

Rhode Island could fit into Alaska, the largest state, 429 times!

Rhode Island Topography

Use the color-coded elevation chart to see on the map Rhode Island's high points (orange) and low points (green to dark green). Elevation is measured as the distance above or below sea level.

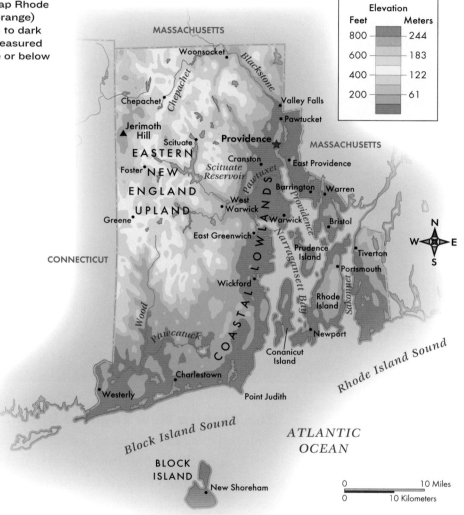

Elevation

Feet	Meters
800	244
600	183
400	122
200	61

Rhode Island is divided into two major land regions. The western half of the state is the Eastern New England Upland. The rest of the state, including the islands that dot Narragansett Bay and the Atlantic Ocean, are part of the Coastal Lowlands.

Boys fishing along the Blackstone River

The Eastern New England Upland

The New England Upland stretches across the northeastern United States and into Canada, and part of its eastern region is located in Rhode Island. This area features forests, rocky hills, and small mountains, along with fertile river valleys that are good for farming. The Blackstone River, which flows from the highlands down into Narragansett Bay, was used to power many of the state's early mills.

In Rhode Island, the elevation of the upland increases from the center of the state to its northwest corner. The town of Foster near the Connecticut border is the site of Jerimoth Hill.

The Coastal Lowlands

The flat Coastal Lowlands region, which borders the Atlantic Ocean, covers much of Rhode Island. Narragansett Bay, a branch of the Atlantic, slices deeply into the eastern part of the state. The bay is 28 miles (45 km) long, and its many inlets and islands contribute to Rhode Island's more than 400 miles (650 km) of coastline. Rocks and cliffs cover much of the bay's shoreline, though the coast along the Atlantic has sandy beaches.

Narragansett Bay has many islands. The city of Newport is on Aquidneck, the largest of these islands. Next to it is Conanicut Island, which is also called Jamestown. Block Island is the state's one main island in the Atlantic. Ferries run to Block Island, a popular vacation spot.

CLIMATE

Summers in Rhode Island tend to be hot and wet. Providence, the state's capital and largest city, has an average high temperature of 83 degrees Fahrenheit (28 degrees Celsius) in July. When summer heat builds,

SEE IT HERE!

MOHEGAN BLUFFS

One of the most striking natural wonders on Block Island is Mohegan Bluffs, cliffs that tower 200 feet (60 m) above the ocean. Glaciers carved the cliffs many thousands of years ago. Since then, the pounding waters of the Atlantic have been eroding, or wearing away, the cliffs. A sandy beach at the base of the bluffs offers a spectacular view.

Weather Report

This chart shows record temperatures (high and low) for the state, as well as average temperatures (July and January) and average annual precipitation.

Record high temperature . . . . 104°F (40°C) at Providence on August 2, 1975
Record low temperature . . . . –25°F (–32°C) at Greene on February 5, 1996
Average July temperature . . . . 73°F (23°C)
Average January temperature . . . . 29°F (–2°C)
Average yearly precipitation . . . . 46 inches (117 cm)

Source: National Climatic Data Center, NESDIS, NOAA, U.S. Dept. of Commerce

THE HURRICANE OF 1938

The trouble started with the rain—days of it. Then the massive storm came ashore. On September 21, 1938, a hurricane packing wind gusts of 175 miles per hour (282 kph) plowed straight into Rhode Island. Along the Atlantic Coast, a wave of water 30 feet (9 m) high crashed into Westerly and nearby towns, killing about 100 people and destroying every building in its path. The wave, called a storm surge, then continued northward into Providence. That surge and overflowing rivers flooded the capital city and other towns in the state. The water tossed boats and cars thousands of feet and even took down brick walls. In the days that followed, thousands of volunteers came to Rhode Island to help residents repair the damage.

Rhode Island is sometimes hit by destructive nor'easters.

Q8 WHAT IS A NOR'EASTER?

A8 A nor'easter is a powerful storm that forms in the Atlantic Ocean and moves up the East Coast of the United States. Most nor'easters occur during the winter months, and the storms typically dump large amounts of rain or snow. The word *nor'easter* is a shortened form of *northeaster*, and it refers to winds that blow out of the northeast during the storm.

thunderstorms sometimes blow in from the west, bringing cooler air. In the winter, snowstorms are frequent. An average of 35 inches (89 centimeters) of snow falls on the state every year.

Large storms called nor'easters sometimes roar up the Atlantic Coast and slam into Rhode Island. During nor'easters, strong winds create pounding waves that erode beaches. A nor'easter in 2006 left some parts of Rhode Island buried under 19 inches (48 cm) of snow. Several deadly hurricanes have also hit Rhode Island.

A nor'easter that hit Rhode Island in February 1978 socked Woonsocket with more than 4 feet (1.2 m) of snow!

Rhode Island's National Park Areas

This map shows some of Rhode Island's national parks, monuments, preserves, and other areas protected by the National Park Service.

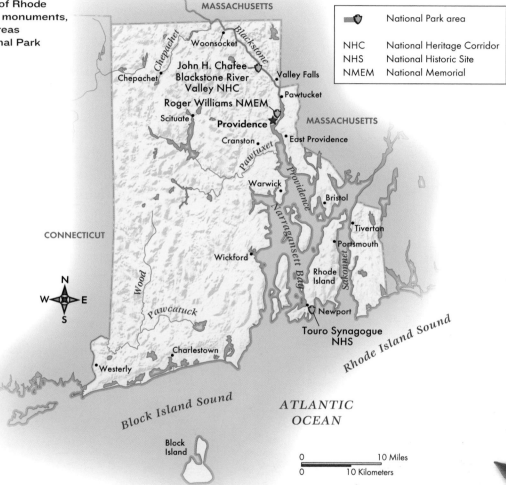

	National Park area
NHC	National Heritage Corridor
NHS	National Historic Site
NMEM	National Memorial

MASSACHUSETTS

Chepachet

Woonsocket

Blackstone

John H. Chafee Blackstone River Valley NHC

Valley Falls

Pawtucket

Roger Williams NMEM

Scituate

Providence

MASSACHUSETTS

Cranston

East Providence

Pawtuxet

Warwick

Bristol

Providence

CONNECTICUT

Tiverton

Portsmouth

Wickford

Sakonnet

Narragansett Bay

Rhode Island

Newport

Touro Synagogue NHS

Rhode Island Sound

N W E S

Pawcatuck

Wood

Charlestown

Westerly

Block Island Sound

ATLANTIC OCEAN

Block Island

0 — 10 Miles
0 — 10 Kilometers

White trillium

PLANT LIFE

The state's upland forests are filled with hardwood trees, including oak, cedar, walnut, and red maple, the state tree. In the fall, the leaves of these trees turn brilliant reds, oranges, and yellows. Wildflowers such as violets, trilliums, and irises also brighten the landscape.

The shore is home to saltmeadow grass, cordgrass, saltwort, and other plants that thrive in wet areas. Marsh lavender has tiny purple flowers that stand out among the green and brown surroundings.

ANIMAL LIFE

Hundreds of different kinds of animals populate Rhode Island. Black bears, deer, and rabbits live in the forest. Otters frolic in Rhode Island's streams, while harbor seals lounge on rocks along the coast. Giant finback, humpback, and right whales swim in the waters near Rhode Island. Sea turtles also make trips to Rhode Island's ocean waters, while smaller turtles make their homes along streams.

Harbor seals rest on Block Island.

A great black-billed gull captures a spider crab at Sachuest Point National Wildlife Refuge, located in Middletown.

WILDLIFE IN DANGER

The U.S. government keeps a list of all wildlife that is in danger of dying out. Rhode Island has just seven animals on that list, but dozens of others could become **endangered** in the future. Rhode Island's endangered species include the Kemp's ridley and leatherback, two sea turtles, and a bug called the American burying beetle. This busy bug buries dead bodies of animals and birds to store them for food. State officials are also concerned about the bobcat, the timber rattlesnake, and several kinds of waterfowl.

Considering the state is nicknamed the Ocean State, you'd expect to find plenty of fish and shellfish in Rhode Island's waters, and you do! Common fish include flounder, sturgeon, and eel. Lobsters as well as clams called quahogs often turn up on dinner tables across the state.

More than 400 different types of birds live in or pass through Rhode Island. Robins and blue jays are common in cities and forests, while laughing loons and majestic egrets stick close to the state's waters. Game birds include partridges and wild turkeys.

Leatherback turtle

WORD TO KNOW

endangered *in danger of becoming extinct*

18

Volunteers for Save the Bay work to preserve eelgrass, an aquatic plant that is nearly extinct in Rhode Island waters.

WORD TO KNOW

reservoir *an artificial lake or tank for storing water*

Water, Water, Everywhere?

Could a state surrounded by water not have enough to drink? That's the question on some Rhode Islanders' minds. The growth of suburbs and industry in the southern part of the state has led some people to call for building a huge new **reservoir**. Homeowners need water to drink, cook, and clean, and some high-tech businesses need huge amounts of water every day. In 2007, Governor Donald Carcieri said, "We must begin to responsibly tap the water resources available in the Big River Reservoir area. This area of our state was set aside in statute as a source of water, and it needs to be accessed now."

Some lawmakers and environmentalists, though, say the solution is not so easy because building the proposed reservoir would cost too much money and harm nearby wetlands. In 2007, state lawmaker J. Michael Lenihan said, "We don't have a crisis at the moment, but one is not far off if we don't do something now." Environmentalists argue that rather than just looking for more water supplies, Rhode Islanders need to reduce the amount of water they use. A good start, some say, is putting limits on watering lawns in the summer, when rivers and reservoirs are at their lowest.

THINK ABOUT IT!

HUMANS AND THE ENVIRONMENT

Wherever people live, they affect the land and water around them. The population of southern Rhode Island has increased dramatically in recent years. The construction of housing developments and office parks can destroy wetlands, and it increases the demand for water.

Human activity poses dangers to Narragansett Bay and the wildlife that relies on it. When humans build near the water, they destroy the homes and food supplies of animals. Pollution from cities and farms also fouls the bay's water.

Since 1970, an organization called Save the Bay has worked to improve the health of Narragansett Bay. Its members have planted marsh grasses that make appealing homes for many kinds of fish. Save the Bay has also stopped the construction of large power plants near the bay. The plants would have produced harmful pollution.

The state's Department of Environmental Management also plays a part in protecting Rhode Island's most precious natural resource. It enforces laws that both limit pollution and protect wildlife in and around the bay.

MINI-BIO

ALLISON ROGERS: ENVIRONMENTAL EDUCATOR

On April 22, 2006, Allison Rogers (1981–) won the Miss Rhode Island crown. It just happened to be Earth Day, a day that honors efforts to keep the environment healthy. Earth Day has special meaning to Rogers. Since her college days, she has worked to reduce global warming, a rise in global temperatures caused by human activity. That warming could threaten animal and plant life around the world. Rogers believes global warming is "the most important issue facing humankind today." As Miss Rhode Island, she toured the state to tell students how they could help, by producing less pollution and reducing energy use. In 2007, she was named Rhode Island's Environmentalist of the Year.

❓ Want to know more?
See http://cao.house.gov/greenthecapitol/alli-rogers.shtml

In recent years, a group called **Clean the Bay** has worked with the state to remove 800 tons of scrap wood and garbage that has washed ashore around Narragansett Bay.

READ ABOUT

Early people in the region learned to hunt with bows and arrows.

c. 13,000 BCE
The last ice age ends in Rhode Island

c. 8000 BCE
The first humans come to Rhode Island

▲ **c. 2500 BCE**
People live in Greenwich Cove on Narragansett Bay

Quahog clams

FIRST PEOPLE

★

FIFTEEN THOUSAND YEARS AGO, THE GLACIERS WERE LEAVING THE AREA THAT WOULD BECOME RHODE ISLAND. At the time, no humans lived in the region. But as the weather slowly warmed, people began arriving in the area. Rhode Island became home to hunters, fishers, gatherers, and later, farmers who relied on the bounty of the land and sea.

c. 1200 CE
Algonquians begin to raise corn

1500
Narragansetts are the dominant people in Rhode Island

c. 500 BCE
The region's first known year-round village is established on Block Island

Archaeologists have found arrowheads and other Native artifacts in Rhode Island.

WORDS TO KNOW

archaeologists *people who study the remains of past human societies*

artifacts *items created by humans, usually for a practical purpose*

When the English came to Rhode Island, they traded with the Native Americans for wampum and sometimes used it as money.

THE FIRST RHODE ISLANDERS

The earliest signs of human life in the region date back about 10,000 years. Hunters and fishers came into southern New England during warmer months seeking food. Near Greenwich Cove on Narragansett Bay, **archaeologists** have found **artifacts** about 4,500 years old. These include stone arrowheads and pieces of pottery.

The first known year-round village in Rhode Island, and perhaps all of New England, was on Block Island. It dates from about 500 BCE. The indigenous, or native, people who lived in this village ate shellfish, seals, and birds. They also gathered wild berries and nuts.

EARLY WAYS OF LIFE

Most of the early people of Rhode Island settled along rivers or the coast. For the groups along Narragansett Bay and the ocean, the quahog clam was an important source of food. Its shell also had great value. Using stone tools, skilled craftsmen drilled beads from purple spots on the shells. These beads, along with white ones made from whelk shells, were called wampum. They were strung together to create belts. The pattern of the beads could be used to record historical events.

Native American Peoples

(Before European Contact)

This map shows the general area of Native American peoples before European settlers arrived.

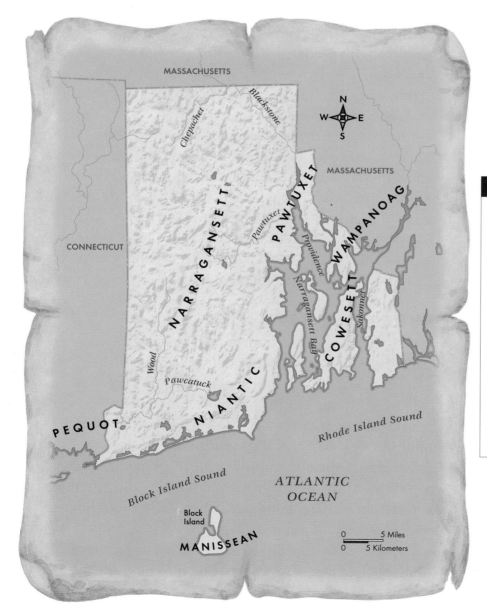

SEE IT HERE!

STONES FROM THE PAST

Early Native Americans in Rhode Island used stone to create long-lasting tools. You can see stone tools that are thousands of years old at the Tomaquag Indian Memorial Museum of Exeter. The museum has a collection of stone arrowheads, spear points, scrapers, and other tools. Tomaquag also features exhibits that describe the life of modern-day Narragansetts from Rhode Island.

Wampum was often exchanged to show good relations between families or groups, and some people were buried with it.

ALGONQUIANS

The Native people of North America spoke many different languages. Algonquian was the major language of groups in what is now the northeastern United States. Various groups in Rhode Island spoke related versions of this language. The people who spoke the Algonquian language are called Algonquian people.

By 1500 CE, Narragansetts, who lived west of the bay eventually named for them, were the largest Native group in Rhode Island. There were about 20,000 of them. The Wampanoag people lived east of the bay and on some of its islands. Their lands extended into what is now Massachusetts. Rhode Island was also home to smaller groups including Niantics, Pawtuxets, and Cowesetts. The Manissean people lived on Block Island.

Native corn

EVERYDAY LIFE

Most Algonquians set up camp in one location for the warmer months, when they hunted, fished, and gathered food. They built small, dome-shaped homes called wigwams, which had stick frames covered with animal skins, tree bark, or mats made from plants. A hole in the top of the wigwam let out the smoke from a fire that kept everyone warm. Most people moved to other camps as the weather turned cold. At these camps, they often built structures called longhouses, which could hold up to 20 families.

Algonquians used boats for fishing and transportation. To build canoes, they cut down trees and used fire to hollow them out. They also made a much lighter type

Algonquians built wigwams from animal skins, sticks, tree bark, and other plant materials.

of canoe by covering a wooden frame with birch bark.

Around 1200 CE, Algonquians learned about corn, a crop they could grow for food. Native people in Mexico had first raised corn several thousand years earlier. Slowly, corn seeds and the knowledge about how to raise corn spread across North America. Soon Algonquians were growing beans and squash as well, and the three crops were sometimes called the "three sisters."

For the Algonquian people of Rhode Island, daily activities often focused on food—finding it, raising it, or preparing it for meals. Men hunted and fished. Sometimes they used nets to trap the fish. They also caught fish using baited hooks. Algonquians had many different methods of hunting. They used bows and arrows to shoot deer,

FAQ

Q8 WHY WERE CORN, BEANS, AND SQUASH CALLED THE "THREE SISTERS"?

A8 The term reflects the close relationship among those crops in an Algonquian field. Algonquians planted corn and bean seeds together in a small mound. The bean plants added nitrogen to the soil. This chemical helped the corn grow. As it grew, the corn supported the vines of the bean plant. The squash was planted in between the mounds. It grew along the ground, helping to stop the growth of weeds.

Picture Yourself . . .

Playing the Fox and the Chicks

You are a Narragansett child. Your daily chores are done, and now it is time for some fun. You gather with your brothers, sisters, and cousins to play games. You start with a race to see who is the fastest. Next, you play a game called the Fox and the Chicks. You and the other "chicks" form a line behind one child called the hen. You hold tightly to the chick in front of you and feel the tight grasp of the chick behind you. Suddenly, the boy or girl who is the fox tries to force you and the other chicks off the line. You try to hold on but cannot. When the last chick is pulled from the hen, the game is over.

Narragansett women had special helpers with their farmwork—tamed hawks! These fast flyers scared away other birds that tried to steal corn or other crops.

geese, and ducks. They set traps to catch foxes and beavers, while they caught turkeys with nets.

When not searching for food, the men made tools out of stone and wood. They also competed in races and shooting contests, played lacrosse and a game similar to soccer, and enjoyed *puim*, which was similar to a card game that used short reeds instead of cards.

Algonquian women raised crops and walked along the shore gathering shellfish. Some women went into the water to catch lobsters. The women smoked and dried the fish that the men caught, preserving it for future meals. Women also built and took down wigwams. Other duties included making mats and clay pots, turning deerskin into leather clothing, and raising children.

Children helped their mothers tend the crops and gather nuts, berries, firewood, and shellfish. As boys grew older, their fathers taught them to hunt. Algonquian children didn't go to school. By watching and listening to the adults around them, they learned about their culture and the proper way to act.

A WORLD OF SPIRITS

The Algonquian people of Rhode Island believed that a sacred force, called *manitou*, filled everything in the universe. They traced both good and bad events—from powerful storms to successful hunts—to this unseen power. Spirits watching over humans also had manitou in them. Algonquians called on these spirits to help during difficult times.

According to Algonquian belief, the water manitou was a giant horned serpent. In the sky, manitou took the form of a creature called the thunderbird. Other beings were thought to have given Algonquians corn and created the rest of the universe.

To contact manitou and the spirit world, Algonquians relied on people called *powwaws*, also known as shamans. Powwaws were thought to learn the future through their dreams. They used medicines made from plants to cure the sick. They also called on the spirits to help cure people. Sometimes, the powwaws smoked tobacco, which was said to help them contact the spirit world. Algonquians also smoked tobacco during important meetings and ceremonies. Among the Algonquian people, tobacco was the only crop raised by men.

Any male Algonquian, not just a powwaw, could seek help from the spirits during a vision quest. In a vision quest, a teenager went out into the woods alone. He neither ate nor drank as he waited for a vision that would guide him in what he should do with his life.

STORYTELLER AND TEACHER

When children today want to know about Rhode Island's distant past, they often gather around Paula "Sunflower" Dove Jennings (1939–). Jennings, who belongs to the Narragansett Nation, is a storyteller who vividly recounts the history of her people. She is the author of the book *Strawberry Thanksgiving*, which explains Narragansett beliefs about how the first strawberries appeared. She has also been a teacher and a member of the Narragansett council.

Native American powwaw

A NEW ERA

In 1500, the Algonquians of Rhode Island were living a mostly peaceful life. They sometimes fought each other, or people who lived farther west, but they had plenty of food and traded with villages hundreds of miles away. Soon, however, the arrival of a new and distant people would change their way of life forever.

READ ABOUT

Giovanni da
Verrazzano's ship
entering Newport
Harbor, 1524

1524

Giovanni da Verrazzano
becomes the first
European known to
reach Rhode Island

▲ 1636
Roger Williams
settles in Providence

1663

Rhode Island receives
a charter from King
Charles II of England

EXPLORATION AND SETTLEMENT

★

ONE DAY IN 1524, WAMPANOAGS IN SMALL BOATS APPROACHED A VESSEL THAT HAD SAILED INTO NARRAGANSETT BAY. From the huge ship, strangely dressed sailors tossed down bells and other small items to the people in the canoes. Sensing the newcomers were friendly, the Native Americans invited them to their village. This pleasant meeting marked the first known arrival of Europeans in the region.

1675
King Philip's War erupts
between Native Americans
and European settlers

1772
Colonists burn the
British ship Gaspee

1790 ▲
Rhode Island becomes
the 13th state to ratify
the U.S. Constitution

European Exploration of Rhode Island

The colored arrows on this map show the routes taken by European explorers from 1524 to 1614.

0 — 5 Miles
0 — 5 Kilometers

Blackstone

Chepachet

Providence

Pawtuxet

Warwick

Providence

Narragansett Bay

Pocasset (Portsmouth)

Sakonnet

Wood

Great Swamp, December, 1675

Newport

Pawcatuck

Rhode Island Sound

ATLANTIC OCEAN

Block Island Sound

Block Island

Giovanni da Verrazzano, 1524	
John Smith, 1614	
Adriaen Block, 1614	
✳	Battle
●	Early settlement
	Present-day state of Rhode Island

WORD TO KNOW

colonies *communities settled in a new land but with ties to another government*

EUROPEAN EXPLORERS

The captain of the ship that reached Rhode Island in 1524 was Giovanni da Verrazzano. He was an Italian sailing for France, which was competing with other European nations to gain **colonies** in the Americas. Since the voyages of Christopher Columbus during the 1490s, Europeans had looked to North and South America for

European settlers building a ship in Narragansett Bay, early 1600s

gold and other precious resources. After Verrazzano's visit, almost 100 years passed before other foreign explorers sailed past Rhode Island or entered its bay.

In 1614, English explorer John Smith sailed all along the New England coast. He drew maps and wrote letters that described its natural beauty. He hoped English settlers would start colonies in the region. The same year, Dutch sea captain Adriaen Block sailed across Long Island Sound. He named an island he saw after himself—Block Island. Neither Smith nor Block actually came ashore in what is now Rhode Island, but just a few years later, English colonists began settling to the north, in Massachusetts. Their settlements—and arguments—would shape the growth of Rhode Island.

When Roger Williams landed in Rhode Island, he was greeted by the Native people.

RELIGIOUS CHANGES

For many centuries, the Roman Catholic Church was the only Christian faith in western Europe. Starting in the early 1500s, however, some people began questioning Catholic practices and founding other churches. They became known as Protestants.

In 1531, England's King Henry VIII broke away from the Catholic Church and started the Church of England. Over the decades, some English Protestants thought the new church did not go far enough in getting rid of Catholic teachings. These Protestants became known as Puritans, because they wanted to purify the Church of England. Other Protestants thought the Church of England could never be a true Christian church. They wanted to separate from it completely, and they became known as Separatists.

In 1620, a group of Separatists left England to form their own colony in Massachusetts, where they could worship as they chose. The Separatists landed in Plymouth, and today they are sometimes called the Pilgrims. In the years that followed, many Puritans left England for Massachusetts. They settled in what are now Salem and Boston and called their colony Massachusetts Bay.

ROGER WILLIAMS ARRIVES

Roger Williams was one of several thousand Puritans who came to Massachusetts Bay during the 1630s. He was a minister, and he took a job at the church in Salem. Soon, however, Williams upset some colonial leaders. He was more of a Separatist than a Puritan. He believed that the government should not dictate a person's religious actions or beliefs. The Puritans ran both the church and the government, and they punished people who did not go to church. Williams believed each person should be allowed to decide what religion to follow. "Forced religion," he said, "stinks in the nostrils of God."

For several years, Williams bounced from town to town in Massachusetts Bay and Plymouth. He angered leaders by attacking Puritan practices. He also stated that England had no legal right to claim land in New England. The land, he said, belonged to the Algonquian people. Fed up with Williams and his ideas, the leaders of Massachusetts Bay **banished** him from the colony. Before he could be sent back to England, Williams fled south, to the land of the Wampanoag Nation.

The Wampanoag people agreed to sell Williams land near the Seekonk River, so he could start a **plantation**. The leaders of Plymouth, however, thought

WORDS TO KNOW

banished *sent out of a place forever*

plantation *a large farm that grows mainly one crop*

Q8 WHO WAS RHODE ISLAND'S FIRST EUROPEAN SETTLER?

A8 William Blackstone was the first European to live in Rhode Island. He moved to Massachusetts in 1623 and then to Rhode Island in 1635, settling in what is now Cumberland. The Blackstone River, which cuts through northeastern Rhode Island, is named for him.

he was too close to their colony, so they asked him to move. He and a few followers then bought land from the Narragansett Nation, at a spot where the Mosshasuck and Woonasquatucket rivers meet. Williams called his new settlement Providence.

Williams had good relations with the Algonquian people. Unlike other Puritan settlers, he respected their right to have their own religion, though he did try to teach them Christian beliefs. He purchased land, while other Europeans tried to take it by force. His friends included Canonicus and Miantonomi, two Narragansett sachems, or leaders. Williams convinced the Narragansett Nation not to join the Pequot people in a war against Puritans in Massachusetts and Connecticut in 1636.

NEW TOWNS

Religious disagreements also prompted other Puritans to leave Massachusetts Bay for Rhode Island. Anne Hutchinson upset Puritan leaders when she challenged their religious authority. Like Williams, she was banished. She moved to Providence in 1638, and with Williams's help, she and her supporters bought Aquidneck Island from the Narragansett people. They called their settlement Pocasset, though they renamed it Portsmouth a few years later. They also renamed their island Rhode Island.

The settlers in Portsmouth included William Coddington. Because of a political dispute, Coddington started a new town on the southern end of the island in 1639. He called it Newport. By the end of the year, almost 100 people lived there.

Another Portsmouth resident who set out on his own was Samuel Gorton. He had been banished from Plymouth, but his beliefs upset leaders in Portsmouth.

Gorton said men and women were completely equal—an uncommon idea at the time. Banished from Portsmouth, Gorton went to Providence before starting a new town, Warwick.

THE CHARTER

The first Rhode Islanders argued over more than just religion. Some Providence settlers wanted more land for themselves, so they split off to form the town of Pawtuxet. The leaders there upset Williams and others when they

ANNE HUTCHINSON: A DARING WOMAN

Anne Hutchinson (1591–1643) and her family reached Boston from England in 1634. Soon she was challenging the local Puritans with her religious ideas. She said a good Christian did not have to follow the rules of a church or of society to go to heaven. Direct, spiritual contact with God was all a believer needed. She was tried before a civil court for teaching her ideas in Boston and was forced out of Massachusetts Bay. After she and her followers founded Portsmouth, Hutchinson moved in 1642 to Long Island, New York. She was killed there the next year during a conflict with Native Americans.

Want to know more? See www.greatwomen.org/women.php?action=viewone&id=84

A view of Portsmouth in 1638

Rhode Island colonists welcomed Roger Williams when he returned with the colonial charter in 1644.

WORDS TO KNOW

charter *a document from a ruler granting rights to a group*

Parliament *the legislature in Great Britain*

declared their loyalty to Massachusetts. Williams knew his Providence Plantation and the other settlements nearby did not have a legal right to exist. Unlike Plymouth and Massachusetts Bay, they didn't have a **charter** from England. To make sure Massachusetts leaders left the Rhode Islanders alone, Williams sailed to England in 1643 to obtain a charter.

At the time, England was in the middle of a civil war. King Charles I was fighting the Puritans who controlled **Parliament**. Williams received a charter from Parliament, which united Providence, Newport, and Portsmouth. Warwick joined the next year, and Pawtuxet became a part of Providence again about a decade later. The charter gave Rhode Islanders the right to run their own local governments. However, the charter didn't spell out the new colony's borders, and this led to decades of conflicts with neighboring Massachusetts and Connecticut.

Still, the colony continued to grow. Its practice of allowing everyone to worship freely drew Quakers, Baptists, and other Protestants who rejected Puritan beliefs. Some Jewish people also began settling in the colony during the 1650s.

LIFE IN THE COLONY

The first settlers in Rhode Island raised corn and beans, crops they had learned about from the Algonquians. The settlers also grew crops they had brought with them from England, such as apples, peas, carrots, and barley. Like the neighboring Indians, the settlers also ate fish from Narragansett Bay and hunted deer and other game. The Rhode Island colonists lived in small wooden houses, though over time the richest settlers built larger homes. Cattle, sheep, and other livestock grazed on the islands of Narragansett Bay. On Aquidneck Island, William Coddington and other wealthy settlers started large farms and hired others to work them. Later, other plantations appeared west of the bay, from Charlestown to Warwick.

The Atlantic Ocean also provided jobs and wealth for Rhode Islanders. Starting around 1670, shipbuilding became a major industry. Rhode Island merchants used these ships to bring farm goods to Boston and to islands in the Caribbean. Newport became a favorite stopping point for pirates who sailed the Atlantic and the Caribbean. The presence of pirates, other criminals, and people with unusual religious views led some New Englanders to call Rhode Island "**Rogue**'s Island."

William Coddington

Captain Kidd, a pirate who visited Rhode Island, may have left buried treasure there. Some folks claim that he left his loot on Block Island or on an island in Narragansett Bay. But no riches have ever been found.

WORD TO KNOW

rogue *a dishonest or worthless person*

NEW CHALLENGES

Although Rhode Islanders had freedom to worship as they chose, they were still tied to Great Britain, and events overseas affected the colony. In 1661, Puritans lost power and Charles II became king. Williams and others worried that the king might not honor the charter of 1643.

However, a new charter from King Charles II in 1663 created the "colony of Rhode Island and Providence Plantations" and provided religious freedom for all. Like the first charter, it gave Rhode Islanders complete control over their local government, as long as their laws did not violate England's. The charter, however, did not solve Rhode Island's border disputes with its neighbors. The current boundaries of Rhode Island were not set until 1747.

KING PHILIP'S WAR

Since the arrival of Roger Williams, life had been mostly peaceful in Rhode Island, thanks to Williams's honest dealings with the Algonquian leaders. But the

The death of Wamsutta, brother of Metacomet

peace was shattered in 1675, when a war between Massachusetts settlers and the Wampanoag Nation spread into Rhode Island. The Wampanoag sachem was named Metacomet, but the English called him King Philip, and the war was named for him. Metacomet went to war after his brother, Wamsutta, died following hours of questioning by the English. The Narragansett people entered the war after Plymouth settlers attacked their camp.

King Philip's War spread across southern New England. During the war, Providence burned, and more than 50 other English towns were attacked. At the same time, several women emerged as Native American leaders. Awashonks, a leader of the Sakonnet Indians, sided with Metacomet for a time but later made a peace agreement with the European settlers. Another Algonquian woman leader during the war was Wetamoo, who was married to Wamsutta. As the colonists pursued her and her people in 1676, Wetamoo drowned trying to escape across the Fall River.

The settlers won the war in the summer of 1676. With their defeat, many Wampanoags and Narragansetts were sold into slavery, including Metacomet's wife and son. King Philip's War marked the last major Indian war in southern New England. The remaining Wampanoags and Narragansetts in Rhode Island were forced to live on a small piece of land near Charlestown. Over time,

MINI-BIO

METACOMET: DEFENDER OF HIS PEOPLE

Metacomet (1639?–1676) was the son of Massasoit, the Wampanoag sachem who had welcomed the Pilgrims when they landed in Plymouth. By the time Metacomet took over as sachem in 1662, the Wampanoag Nation had lost much of its land to the newcomers. In 1675, Metacomet fought the English to preserve what was left of Indian land and culture. During King Philip's War, Metacomet rode a black horse, a gift from the English during friendlier days. He rode as far as New York to escape capture, before returning to his camp in Bristol, Rhode Island, where he was killed by a Native American working for the English.

❓ **Want to know more?** See www.tolatsga.org/wampa.html

Q8 WHO WAS THE BLACK "GOVERNOR" OF RHODE ISLAND?

A8 White masters allowed enslaved Africans to have an "election day" in which they would elect one person as their so-called governor. The governor was respected among the enslaved people, and he had the power to punish slaves who harmed other slaves. But he had no legal power over white Rhode Islanders. Election Day became a huge celebration, with music and food.

WORD TO KNOW

smuggle *to bring in or take out illegally*

In the southern part of the state, enslaved Africans tended cattle and sheep and worked on dairy farms. In the northern part, they worked as house servants, craftspeople, and sailors. Enslaved people in Rhode Island had some legal rights. Some had a chance to earn money, and a few were able to buy their freedom. They could testify in court against white people and challenge jurors in their own cases. Enslaved people in the southern colonies lacked these rights. Still, enslaved Africans often tried to escape. Many ran away with enslaved Indians or with white indentured servants. So many people ran away that as early as 1710, the colony's laws called for severely punishing escaped slaves who were caught and any whites who helped them.

THE ROAD TO REVOLUTION

Starting at the end of the 17th century, Great Britain and France fought several wars as they competed to control North America. The last of these, called the French and Indian War (1754–63), ended with a British victory, giving that country almost all of France's lands east of the Mississippi River. Soon after the war, King George III decided Great Britain needed to raise money in the colonies to pay its debts and keep soldiers in North America.

In 1764, Great Britain passed the Sugar Act. This law made it harder for Rhode Islanders to **smuggle** molasses and sugar from the West Indies, as they had in the past, to avoid paying taxes. More British ships patrolled Narragansett Bay, and smugglers who were caught faced trial outside the colony. The British action threatened to destroy the colony's rum industry. Governor Stephen Hopkins was one of the first Americans to protest taxes on the colonies. He said Parliament did not

The burning of the *Gaspee*, a British ship, in Narragansett Bay, 1772

have a right to tax them because the Americans had no elected officials representing their interests.

Anger over British policies grew the next year, when Parliament passed the Stamp Act. The law placed a tax on paper goods and documents used in the colonies. Mobs stormed the homes of three Rhode Islanders who supported the king. The British did not enforce the new law, but in the following years they passed other taxes on the colonies. In Newport, tensions rose when the British forced local sailors to work on their ships. The bad feelings grew in 1772, when some Providence residents burned the *Gaspee*, a British naval ship, after it ran aground near Warwick.

The first circus in the American colonies was founded in Newport in 1774. It featured trick horse-riding.

WORDS TO KNOW

patriots *Americans who supported independence from Great Britain*

privateers *private citizens given government approval to capture enemy ships*

Patriot troops carrying gunpowder near Portsmouth, 1775

BATTLE FOR INDEPENDENCE

In April 1775, British troops stationed in Boston clashed with Massachusetts **patriots**. Their battles marked the start of the American Revolution. Rhode Island soon sent troops to help fight the British, though some local residents did remain loyal to the king. In June 1775, a small Rhode Island fleet captured a British ship, and local **privateers** captured many more ships throughout the war.

In July 1776, the United States officially declared its independence from Great Britain. Patriots in Newport celebrated the news, but the cheering was over by December, when the British took over the city and other parts of southern Rhode Island. British troops raided local farms for food, cut down trees for firewood, and burned many homes.

Rhode Island: From Territory to Statehood
(1763–1790)

This map shows many of the colonies and the area that became the state of Rhode Island in 1790.

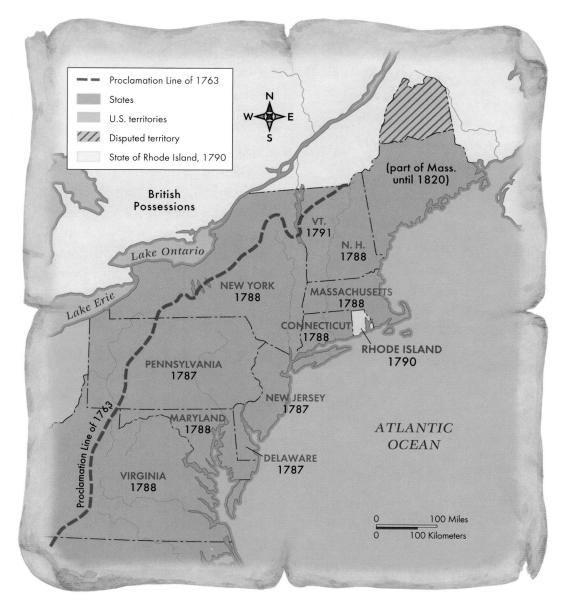

Legend:
- Proclamation Line of 1763
- States
- U.S. territories
- Disputed territory
- State of Rhode Island, 1790

British Possessions

Lake Ontario

Lake Erie

VT. 1791

N. H. 1788

NEW YORK 1788

MASSACHUSETTS 1788

(part of Mass. until 1820)

CONNECTICUT 1788

RHODE ISLAND 1790

PENNSYLVANIA 1787

NEW JERSEY 1787

MARYLAND 1788

DELAWARE 1787

VIRGINIA 1788

Proclamation Line of 1763

ATLANTIC OCEAN

0 100 Miles
0 100 Kilometers

MINI-BIO

NATHANAEL GREENE: PATRIOT

During the Revolution, no Rhode Islander did more for the American cause than Nathanael Greene (1742–1786). Born in Potowomut, he had no military experience when he was named a major general in 1776. But he strongly supported the struggle for independence and eagerly did whatever he could to help. For a time, he located food and supplies for the troops. His greatest fame, however, came on the battlefield, where he led the Americans to victory in several key battles in the South. After the war, Georgia rewarded him for his efforts by giving him land, and he died in that state.

❓ **Want to know more?** See www.georgiaencyclopedia.org/nge/Article.jsp?id=h-2556

WOW

The largest land battle of the American Revolution in New England took place near Newport in August 1778. Between 12,000 and 15,000 soldiers took part in the Battle of Rhode Island.

To fight back, some Rhode Islanders carried out a daring raid of their own. On July 9, 1777, Colonel William Barton led a group of men who captured British general George Prescott from a house in Portsmouth where he sometimes stayed. The Americans later swapped Prescott for one of their own generals who had been captured by the British.

Rhode Island was one of many colonies that recruited both black and white men to fight in the Continental army. General Nathanael Greene's First Regiment was a unit of more than 120 black men, including almost 100 enslaved Africans. Members of the First Regiment fought bravely during the Battle of Rhode Island.

A NEW GOVERNMENT

The war finally ended in 1783. Rhode Island was now one of the 13 U.S. states. Its residents, though, had paid a high price for independence. The British had devastated Newport, Rhode Island's largest city at the time. Several thousand people had fled, and many resettled in Providence.

Many Rhode Islanders feared losing some of the independence they had just won to the new U.S. government. In 1787, when other states called for a convention to create a stronger national government, Rhode Island did not take part. The convention ended

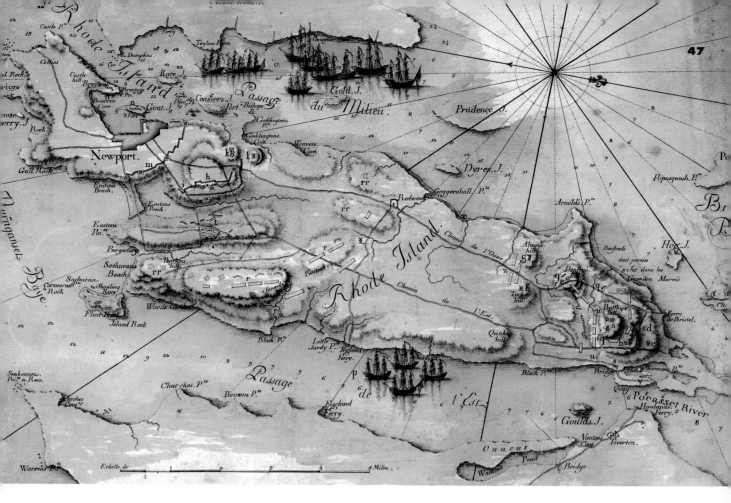

with the drafting of the **Constitution**, which created the U.S. government still used today.

As the other states began to ratify, or approve, the Constitution, Rhode Island lawmakers refused to consider it. James Madison, who helped write the Constitution, once complained about the "wickedness and folly" that seemed to grip Rhode Island's leaders. But many Rhode Island business owners liked the fact that the new national government was going to pay state debts from the war. Finally, in 1790, the state's merchants and a visit from George Washington, who had led the Continental army during the war, convinced the state's lawmakers to ratify the Constitution. Rhode Island was now the 13th state in the Union.

This map of the Battle of Rhode Island shows the position of French ships and the American army under the command of General John Sullivan in 1778.

WORD TO KNOW

Constitution *the written document that contains all the governing principles of the United States*

48

READ ABOUT

Providence in 1827

▲**1793**
*Samuel Slater opens the
first mechanized textile
mill in the United States*

1833
*Workers begin
building a railroad
across the state*

1841
*Thomas Dorr leads
a rebellion over
voting rights*

CHAPTER FOUR

GROWTH AND CHANGE

★

THE RUSH OF WATER OVER A WOODEN WHEEL, THE HUM OF MACHINES—THESE WERE THE SOUNDS OF RHODE ISLAND IN THE EARLY 19TH CENTURY. The state became a national leader in building mills and factories, and it attracted many thousands of immigrants to work in them.

1860s ►

Elizabeth Buffum Chace harbors runaway slaves

1888

The law is changed so that immigrants can vote in statewide elections without owning property

1917

Thousands of Rhode Islanders join the military to fight in World War I

PIONEERING ACTIVIST

Occramar Marycoo (1746–1826) was a teenager when he left his native Ghana for North America. A sea captain had promised to take the young African there so he could go to school. Instead, the captain sold Marycoo into slavery in Rhode Island, and the teen was renamed Newport Gardner. In Newport, he used his skills as a musician to earn money and buy his freedom. He continued his musical career, but he also worked hard to help other free Africans. In 1780, he started the African Union Society, and later he started a school for black children and Newport's first church for blacks. Gardner, however, lost faith that Africans would ever receive equal treatment in the United States, and he returned to Africa shortly before his death.

NEW WAYS TO WEALTH

After the American Revolution, Rhode Island granted several hundred enslaved Africans their freedom for fighting in the war. It also passed a law that children born to slaves after March 1, 1784, would be free. Then, in 1787, a state law ended the slave trade. Rhode Island merchants, however, were not willing to end their trade in slaves. Some sailed to and from ports in other states, and others smuggled slaves. The wealthy Brown family of Providence was deeply divided over the slave trade. Moses Brown took his brother John to court because he continued to bring slaves to the state.

Shippers who didn't want to break the law found a booming business trading goods in China and other parts of Asia. They brought back items such as tea, coffee, silk, china dishes, and fabrics. Robert Gray of Tiverton led the way, reaching China in 1789. His ship, the *Columbia Rediviva*, became the first American vessel to sail completely around the world when it returned to New England.

After 1790, however, a new industry offered investors another way to make money. That year, Samuel Slater arrived in Rhode Island from England. He came with plans for building the most advanced spinning machine of the day. Until then, only the British used the machines to spin cotton thread. The rest of the world still did the job by hand. Moses Brown and his partner invested money so Slater could build a textile factory in Pawtucket, the first ever in the United States. It opened in 1793, and others soon followed. The rivers in the northeastern corner of Rhode Island powered waterwheels that turned the machines in the factories. By 1815, the state had 100 cotton mills, and wool mills soon opened, too. Steam engines slowly replaced water-

This cotton mill was established on the Blackstone River by Samuel Slater in 1793.

wheels as the mills' source of power. With these factories, the American Industrial Revolution was born.

ANOTHER WAR

As Rhode Island began to industrialize, more trouble was brewing. Wars between France and Great Britain affected American shippers. The Americans wanted to trade with both sides, but the French and British did not want them trading with their enemy. The situation finally led to the War of 1812, another war between the United States and Great Britain. Most Rhode Islanders opposed

FAQ

Q8 WHAT WAS THE INDUSTRIAL REVOLUTION?

A8 The Industrial Revolution was a period when industry replaced farming as the main source of jobs. It began in the 18th century in England. During the Industrial Revolution, waterpower, steam engines, and finally electric- and gas-powered engines replaced animals and humans as the main source of power for most tasks.

It was not unusual for children to work long hours in textile mills in Rhode Island and other states.

the war, because they made most of their money trading with the British. In 1814, some even talked about joining the other New England states in leaving the Union. But Rhode Island remained a state, and the war ended in 1815.

AN INDUSTRIAL STATE

In the two decades after the War of 1812, more Rhode Island investors turned to manufacturing. In addition to producing textiles, state workers crafted the spinning machines and looms used in the factories in Rhode Island and other states. The state also became a center for making jewelry and silver goods. Providence became the financial and transportation center of the state.

As more money went into building factories in Rhode Island, the shipping trade almost completely dried up. Newport and other coastal towns lost jobs. Farming also became less important, as people left the land to work in the mills.

Many of the textile workers were women and children. Millwork gave young women their first chance to leave their small towns and have some independence. But in the mills, they faced long hours and dangerous work conditions for low pay. Children suffered even more from millwork. Rhode Island's first public school system began in the 1820s, but many children went to the mills rather than school. They needed to make money for their families. In some textile mills, half the workers were children.

The rise of industry also brought many immigrants to Rhode Island. The Irish started coming in the 1820s. They worked in the mills and helped build the Blackstone Canal, which connected Providence to the industrial city of Worcester, Massachusetts. Starting in 1833, they also worked building railroads in the state. During the 1860s, French Canadians began heading south to Rhode Island. Like the Irish, they were mostly Roman Catholic, while most native-born Rhode Islanders were Protestant. Because of this, the new arrivals sometimes faced **prejudice**. Many companies ran ads saying "No Irish need apply." The French Canadians also struggled to fit in because they didn't speak English.

Narragansetts who remained in the state also faced prejudice. For several decades, they had not been allowed to run their own government on their lands in Charlestown. And white Americans expected them to give up their traditional culture and live as they did.

Prejudice against African Americans was even stronger. In 1822, a state law barred them from voting,

In 1824, textile mill workers in Pawtucket went on **strike** when mill owners tried to cut wages by 25 percent. Never before had women taken part in a strike in the United States.

WORDS TO KNOW

strike *an organized refusal to work, usually as a sign of protest about working conditions*

prejudice *an unreasonable hatred or fear of others*

and in 1824 and 1831, whites rioted against peaceful black communities. In Providence, the black community fought back against the rioters.

THE DORR REBELLION

Immigration and a changing economy led to political troubles in Rhode Island. In the 1840s, the charter of 1663 was still the supreme law of the state. Unlike the other colonies, Rhode Island had not written a constitution when it became a state. The charter limited voting to male landowners, making Rhode Island one of few states that still did not allow all white men to vote. This upset many Rhode Islanders. Most immigrants and mill workers didn't own land, so they couldn't vote. The voting restrictions also affected merchants and artisans whose jobs didn't require land.

Because of these rules, more than half of the adult white men in Rhode Island could not vote. Free blacks had lost the right to vote in 1822, and women could not vote either. The charter also gave the state's rural towns vastly greater representation in the General Assembly, the state's lawmaking body, than the rapidly growing towns in the industrial corner of the state.

Some Rhode Islanders began to demand an end to these unfair arrangements, and Thomas Dorr, a wealthy lawyer and lawmaker, emerged as their leader. Dorr's supporters formed the People's Party and held statewide elections. Dorr was elected governor. In 1841, he and his supporters drafted their own constitution that would have allowed all white men to vote.

Meanwhile, Samuel Ward King of the Law and Order Party was elected governor

Thomas Dorr

under the charter. For a time, the state had two elected governments. Dorr's was illegal, but it had the support of many Rhode Islanders. In 1842, supporters of the People's Party prepared to fight supporters of the Law and Order Party. Dorr led an assault on the Providence arsenal, where weapons were stored. The attack failed, and Dorr briefly fled the state.

The so-called Dorr Rebellion ended when the Law and Order Party wrote a constitution in 1843. Under this constitution, native-born men, both black and white, were allowed to vote without owning property. This constitution also gave cities more members in the General Assembly, the state's lawmaking body. Immigrants, however, still faced severe limits on their voting rights. Foreign-born U.S. citizens who did not own property could not vote in state or national elections.

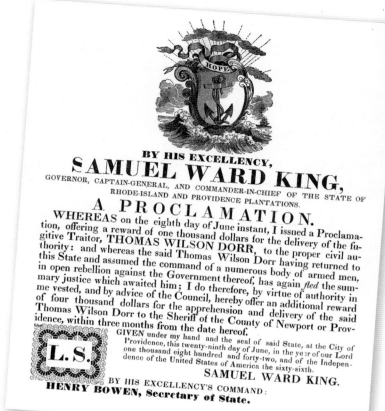

Samuel Ward King issued this proclamation calling Thomas Dorr a traitor.

THE CIVIL WAR

By 1860, the United States was deeply divided over the issue of slavery. Many Southerners, even some who did not own slaves, believed slavery was necessary to keep their plantations and businesses running. Many Northerners opposed the spread of slavery into new states and territories, and a smaller number were abolitionists, people who wanted to end slavery entirely. Elizabeth Buffum Chace of Smithfield harbored runaway slaves and helped organize an antislavery society.

Colonel Ambrose Burnside (seated center) and members of the 1st Rhode Island Infantry Regiment in 1861

FAQ ★ ★ ★

Q8 WHAT IS AMBROSE BURNSIDE BEST KNOWN FOR?

A8 Burnside grew long tufts of hair on either side of his face. After the Civil War, similar facial hair was called "sideburns" in his honor, and the term is still used today.

But Rhode Island textile mills used Southern cotton as their raw material, and some Southerners vacationed in Newport. With those ties, the state did not have a strong abolitionist movement.

However, when Southern states began leaving the Union in December 1860, sparking the Civil War, Rhode Islanders wanted to keep the Union whole. When the actual fighting began the next April, young Rhode Island men of both races volunteered to fight for the Union. About 1,800 African American Rhode Islanders fought in all-black units with white officers.

Rhode Island resident Ambrose Burnside rose to the rank of general and led Union troops at several key battles. Governor William Sprague also served as an officer. And Kady Brownell was one of a handful of women who fought during the Civil War. Brownell followed her husband from Providence to the battlefield and trained with the soldiers. She was the only woman to receive discharge papers from the government after her military service. But she represented the kind of service thousands of New England women were ready to offer to ensure a Union victory.

BOOM TIMES

The Civil War ended in 1865 with a Northern victory. Rhode Islanders went back to work in the state's many textile mills and other factories. The men who owned the factories continued to control Rhode Island politics, and **corruption** was common. Party leaders paid voters to elect their candidates, and some state officials used their positions to make money illegally. The idea of Rhode Island as "Rogue's Island" continued.

But the war had also been a time of racial progress. When the war started, Providence, Newport, and Bristol still sent blacks and whites to separate schools. Less than six months after the war ended, Newport **integrated** its schools. Then in 1866, the state integrated all its schools.

In the decades after the Civil War, Rhode Island became a popular vacation spot for wealthy people from across the East. With its rich sailing heritage, Rhode Island also became a center for building and sailing pleasure boats. Newport drew the richest of the rich, and some built huge mansions they called "cottages." Westerly, Jamestown, Narragansett, and Block Island also attracted tourists, not all of them wealthy. Coastal towns built amusement parks and boardwalks

MINI-BIO

ELIZABETH BUFFUM CHACE: A FIGHTER FOR RIGHTS

Elizabeth Buffum Chace (1806–1899) was a Quaker, a member of a Christian group that supported the idea that all people are equal. The Smithfield native married a wealthy cotton mill owner and then spent decades campaigning to end slavery and help women gain the right to vote. She also worked to improve conditions in women's prisons and helped start a school for homeless children. In 2001, Rhode Island put a statue of Chace in the capitol, making her the first woman to receive that honor.

? Want to know more? See www.quahog.org/factsfolklore/index.php?id=104

WORDS TO KNOW

corruption *illegal or unfair acts committed by government or business officials*

integrated *brought together all members of society*

SEE IT HERE!

THE BREAKERS

Of all the grand Newport mansions, none was grander than the Breakers. The stone home was built by Cornelius Vanderbilt II, whose family had made a fortune in steamships and railroads. In 1893, work began on the house, which was modeled after 16th-century Italian mansions. When it was done, the Breakers featured 70 rooms, including a "great hall" with ceilings 45 feet (14 m) high. Visitors to Newport can tour this and other nearby mansions.

MINI-BIO

IDA LEWIS: LIGHTHOUSE KEEPER

Ida Lewis (1842–1911), who was born in Newport, was the keeper of the Lime Rock Lighthouse in Newport Harbor for nearly 50 years. During that time, she rescued at least 17 people, including six soldiers, from drowning. Her father had been the lighthouse keeper, and she took over unofficially after he became ill in the late 1850s. The government did not make her the official keeper until 1879. Two years later, she received a medal from the U.S. Lighthouse Service for her heroics.

Want to know more? See www.nps.gov/history/maritime/keep/keephero.htm

The Breakers mansion in Newport

for average people looking for fun on their day off from work. Lighthouses were constructed along the coast to keep boaters safe.

An Italian family inside their home in Providence, late 1800s

NEW ARRIVALS, OLD PROBLEMS

With Rhode Island's many factories constantly humming, more immigrants came to the state looking for jobs. French Canadians continued to flock there, taking unskilled jobs in mills. Skilled textile workers from the British Isles often managed the mills. After 1880, more immigrants arrived from Italy, Portugal, Poland, and eastern Europe. The constant stream of immigrants helped push the population of Providence from 54,595 in 1865 to 175,597 in 1900. Pawtucket and Woonsocket were also thriving factory cities.

Newcomers continued to face restrictions on voting. In 1888, an amendment, or change, to the state constitution finally gave immigrants the right to vote for city mayors and in national and statewide elections, even if they didn't own property. But no one who lived in a city—natives or immigrants—could vote for local lawmakers unless they owned property. Many immigrants needed their wages to support their families or to send back home to relatives. Saving enough to buy property could take a long time, so about 60 percent of Rhode Island's city residents were shut out of local elections.

Other laws gave the state senate the power to choose most nonelected government officials. The senate still gave rural towns more power than cities, where most immigrants lived. For the first few decades of the 20th century, businesses and rural residents controlled Rhode Island politics, shutting out factory workers and immigrants.

The state's first settlers, the Narragansett people, also struggled in these years. In 1880, the state said the Narragansett Nation was no longer an official tribe, so state residents could start buying Narragansett lands. The remaining Narragansett people began taking jobs and living in nearby towns, but they never stopped their fight to regain their lands.

These members of the Rhode Island Women's League, photographed in 1900, fought for voting rights and other women's issues.

Navy recruits boarding a train in Newport, 1917

A WORLD AT WAR

By the early 1900s, the Rhode Island economy began to lose some steam. Companies could make textiles cheaper in southern states, where wages were lower.

In 1917, the United States entered World War I, which was already raging in Europe. The United States joined on the side of Great Britain, France, and other nations that were fighting Germany and its **allies**. Thousands of Rhode Islanders soon found jobs working for the U.S. government or companies that supplied the troops. The government trained sailors for merchant ships in Newport, and Goat Island was the home of the Naval Torpedo Station. Several thousand workers there, including 300 women, helped build weapons to destroy German submarines.

The war ended with a German defeat in 1918. Rhode Islanders hoped for better days to come.

WORD TO KNOW

allies *people who are on the same side in a conflict*

READ ABOUT

Men and boys prepare to start their workday at the Warren Manufacturing Company, early 1900s

1922
Isabelle Ahearn O'Neill becomes the first female lawmaker in Rhode Island

1933 ▲
Theodore Francis Green is elected governor and later takes part in the Bloodless Revolution

1950
Providence is home to nearly 250,000 people

CHAPTER FIVE

MORE MODERN TIMES

★

IN THE 1920s, MOST OF THE COUNTRY ENJOYED THE ROARING TWENTIES. As the U.S. economy boomed, people danced to jazz music, listened to the first radios, and watched the first films with sound. But for Rhode Island, the 1920s were more of a whimper than a roar. Industries struggled, and politicians battled. The rogues still seemed to be in control.

▲ **1978**
The Narragansett Nation wins back its land in Charlestown

1980–2000
Rhode Island's Hispanic population quadruples

early 1990s
Providence enjoys a "Renaissance"

MINI-BIO

THEODORE FRANCIS GREEN: "REVOLUTIONARY" GOVERNOR

Theodore Francis Green (1867–1966) was a rarity in Rhode Island politics: a wealthy, white Protestant who was also a Democrat. He was elected governor in 1933, and in 1935 he took part in what has been called the Bloodless Revolution. Green and his supporters managed to overturn the election of two Republicans to the state senate. Their success gave the Democrats control of both houses in the General Assembly, and they soon filled the state supreme court and other parts of the state government with Democrats. These moves gave the Democrats control over Rhode Island politics for years to come. After serving as governor, Green represented Rhode Island in the U.S. Senate for 24 years.

? Want to know more? See http://bioguide.congress.gov/scripts/biodisplay.pl?index=G000418

Politics was sometimes dirty in Rhode Island—and smelly too! In 1924, Republicans hired a crook to set off a stink bomb in the General Assembly, hoping to end a debate on an issue important to the Democrats.

TOUGH TIMES

After World War I, Rhode Island's textile industry continued its decline. Companies fired workers, cut wages, or shut down completely. At times, workers went on strike to demand better pay, but the industry was dying in the state where it had been born. And few new companies appeared to replace the lost jobs.

Throughout these years, Rhode Island's political leaders squabbled with each other. The Republican Party had controlled the state for decades, but during the 1920s, Democrats won the support of immigrant voters and began to take over. They managed to give larger towns more representatives in the state senate. They also finally ended the property requirement to vote in local elections. With that change, the Democrats were able to win many elections in cities and towns. During the 1930s, many Democrats of Irish, French Canadian, and Italian descent got government positions, replacing Republicans with British roots.

In 1935, Governor Theodore Francis Green solidified Democratic control in what became known as the Bloodless Revolution. Green replaced all the Republicans on the state supreme court and replaced many other Republican government appointees. Since

Mill workers on strike in Pawtucket, 1922

that time, Democrats have been the dominant party in the state.

FROM BAD TO WORSE

In 1929, the entire United States entered the Great Depression, the worst economic downturn in the country's history. Banks failed, businesses closed, and people lost their jobs. Strikes were common. In September 1934, textile workers clashed with police, leaving three people dead. Governor Green finally called in the National Guard to end the strike. By 1937, many of the state's textile mills had closed for good.

In 1932, Americans elected Franklin D. Roosevelt president. The next year, he began the

POLITICAL LEADER

In 1920, women across the United States won the right to vote. Two years later, Isabelle Ahearn O'Neill (1880–1975) became the first woman to serve in the Rhode Island General Assembly. O'Neill, the daughter of Irish immigrants, was born in Woonsocket. Before entering politics, she had acted in several silent films and taught in Providence. During part of her eight years in the Rhode Island House of Representatives, she served as a Democratic Party leader. She went on to serve two years in the state senate. In 1933, President Franklin D. Roosevelt named her to a U.S. agency that fought illegal drug use. O'Neill is remembered today as a pioneering female politician.

The postwar years saw the first interstate highways crisscross Rhode Island. They made it easier for people to work in the city and drive home to the suburbs at night. As new shopping centers and malls opened in the suburbs, many Providence department stores closed their doors. The new highways also greatly reduced travel times to Boston, Massachusetts. Many Rhode Islanders began traveling to Boston to work at higher-paying jobs.

The state's economy suffered throughout this period. Many factories moved out of state or closed their doors entirely. For a time, the U.S. Navy provided jobs, but in 1973, the navy moved part of its fleet out of Newport, putting 16,000 people out of work. In the decades after World War II, Rhode Islanders faced higher unemployment and lower wages than workers in many parts of the country. Many businesses avoided Rhode Island because the state had higher taxes than other states, and lawmakers were thought to favor workers over businesses.

Meanwhile, corruption plagued Rhode Island politics during the 1980s and 1990s. Several government officials, including Providence mayor Buddy Cianci, a state supreme court judge, and Governor Edward D. DiPrete, were convicted of crimes.

RHODE ISLAND TODAY

Rhode Islanders are optimistic about their state. Since the late 1970s, state, federal, and private money have been used to reinvigorate Providence. Cianci led the city through what is called the Providence Renaissance (*Renaissance* means "rebirth") in the early 1990s. The city cleaned up its waterfront and uncovered three rivers that had been buried beneath streets and buildings. These days, Providence has a new convention center and a thriving arts scene.

In recent years, the Narragansett people have reemerged as a visible force in Rhode Island. In 1978, they won a court battle that gave them 1,800 acres (728 hectares) of their former land in Charlestown. On their new reservation, they promote schooling and jobs for their members.

Today, Rhode Island continues to be a magnet for immigrants, particularly from Portugal, Asian nations, and Spanish-speaking countries. Hispanics began arriving in large numbers during the 1970s, and between 1980 and 2000, the state's Hispanic population quadrupled. Most settled in and around Providence, where they found work in factories or restaurants. These days, people of many different backgrounds think their little state has a big future.

WaterFire along the Providence River

SEE IT HERE!

WATERFIRE

As part of the Providence Renaissance, Barnaby Evans created a sculpture titled *WaterFire* in 1994. The sculpture consists of 100 metal baskets sitting on posts in the rivers that had been uncovered. Several nights a year, the baskets are filled with wood logs that are set ablaze. The flames, their reflections, and the city skyline create a striking sight. Music plays along the riverbanks as the fires burn through the night. *WaterFire* has drawn visitors from around the world and is among the brightest signs of Providence's continuing importance to Rhode Island.

70

READ ABOUT

Young people enjoying time at a playground

CHAPTER SIX

PEOPLE

★

MORE THAN 1 MILLION PEOPLE ARE PACKED INTO THE TINY STATE OF RHODE ISLAND, MOST OF THEM IN OR NEAR PROVIDENCE. An average of almost 1,013 people live in each square mile (391 per sq km), making Rhode Island the second most densely populated state in the country after New Jersey. But most Rhode Islanders don't mind. One advantage of living in a small state is that no matter where you are, pockets of quiet countryside or wide sandy beaches are never too far away.

Big City Life

This list shows the population of Rhode Island's biggest cities

Providence	.176,862
Warwick	87,233
Cranston	.81,614
Pawtucket	.73,742
East Providence	.49,515

Source: U.S. Census Bureau, 2006 estimate

AT HOME IN RHODE ISLAND

Providence is the largest city in Rhode Island. The four next-largest cities are near Providence. The state's smallest towns lie along the border with Connecticut and the southern shore. Even these areas, though, are close enough to cities to be called urban areas.

WHO'S A RHODE ISLANDER?

Over the centuries, people from all over the world have settled in Rhode Island. Today's residents trace their roots to dozens of countries. Topping the list is Ireland, followed

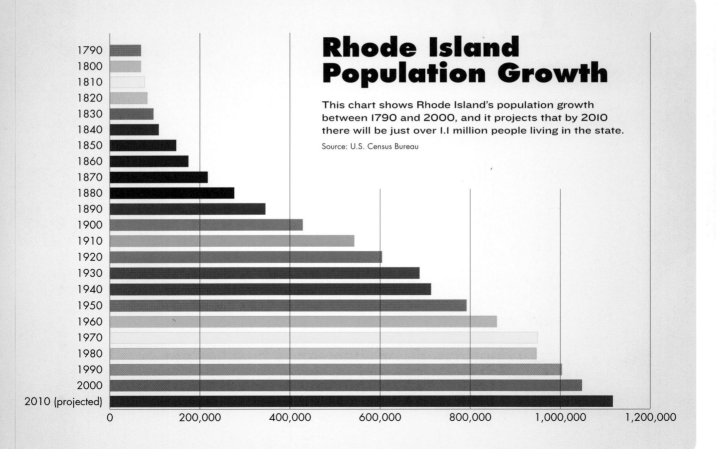

Rhode Island Population Growth

This chart shows Rhode Island's population growth between 1790 and 2000, and it projects that by 2010 there will be just over 1.1 million people living in the state.

Source: U.S. Census Bureau

A family in Providence

closely by Italy. Both Irish and Italian Americans have been important in state politics. Many Rhode Islanders also trace their roots to England, French Canada, and Portugal. English settlers helped turn Rhode Island from a colony to a state, while French Canadians worked in the mills. Nearly 9 percent of Rhode Islanders are of Portuguese descent—the highest percentage of any state in the country. Many Portuguese have worked as fishers along the state's shores.

Rhode Islanders harvest almost 4 million pounds (1.8 million kilograms) of quahog clams every year, about one-quarter of the total amount harvested in the entire United States.

HOW TO TALK LIKE A RHODE ISLANDER

Traveling across Rhode Island, you're bound to hear some words or expressions that leave you a little confused. If you're dying for a drink, a Rhode Islander might direct you to a bubbler—the state's word for a water fountain. And Rhode Islanders love to drink coffee-flavored milk shakes, which they call coffee cabinets. Want a long, meat-stuffed sandwich to go with that? Ask for a grinder, which in other parts of the United States is a sub, a hero, or a hoagie. Would you rather have a hot dog? Then go to a weiner place. If all these things are on sale, Rhode Islanders say they're on special.

HOW TO EAT LIKE A RHODE ISLANDER

For centuries, Rhode Islanders have looked to the sea and Narragansett Bay for some of their favorite foods. That love of fish and shellfish continues today. Many Rhode Islanders enjoy clambakes, which feature clams, lobster, corn, and potatoes all cooked together, either on a stove or outdoors over hot rocks, wood coals, and seaweed. The first clambakes took place long before the English came to Rhode Island, when Algonquian Indians roasted clams, oysters, and lobsters over hot stones.

Italian immigrants brought their love of food to Rhode Island, and pizzerias and Italian restaurants are found all over the state. A *wandi*—deep-fried pastry—is a common treat. These sweet treats are sometimes called doughboys.

Lobster, clams, corn, and melted butter at a clambake

MENU

WHAT'S ON THE MENU IN RHODE ISLAND?

Rhode Island Clam Chowder

All clam chowders feature bits of clams, potatoes, and vegetables in a broth, but only Rhode Islanders serve it in a clear broth. Typical Rhode Island chowder uses quahogs.

Stuffies

A stuffy is a baked quahog clam stuffed with bread crumbs, herbs, and sometimes bacon or a sausage called chorizo.

Coffee Syrup

Rhode Island is the coffee syrup capital of the United States, since it's home to the only company that makes it. This sweet, coffee-flavored liquid is added to milk to make the official state drink—coffee milk. The syrup is also a key ingredient in a coffee cabinet.

Frozen Lemonade

Need to cool off on a hot day? Then try one of Rhode Island's favorite summertime treats: frozen lemonade. Shavings of ice are mixed with bits of fresh lemons and sugar.

Dynamite

The small northern town of Woonsocket is home to one explosive sandwich—the dynamite. Hamburger, peppers, onions, and tomato sauce are mixed together to create a sloppy, spicy filling for long rolls.

TRY THIS RECIPE
Johnnycakes

When is a pancake not a pancake? When it's made in Rhode Island and called a johnnycake. These Rhode Island specialties are made with cornmeal rather than flour. Have an adult nearby when you make this recipe.

Ingredients:
1 cup cornmeal
½ teaspoon salt
2 teaspoons sugar (optional)
1 to 1½ cups boiling water
3 tablespoons milk
3 tablespoons vegetable oil (or bacon fat)

Instructions:
1. Mix together all the dry ingredients in a bowl.
2. Use a whisk to stir in the boiling water until the mixture is mushy.
3. Whisk in the milk until the batter is smooth.
4. Heat a heavy frying pan over medium-high heat and add the oil or fat.
5. Spoon out enough of the mixture onto the pan to make a cake about ¼ inch thick and 3 inches wide.
6. Cook each side for about 4 to 5 minutes, until brown.
7. Serve the johnnycakes with maple syrup and butter.

Stuffies

Frozen lemonade

MINI-BIO

EDWARD BANNISTER: PRIZE-WINNING PAINTER

Edward Bannister (1828–1901) was born in Canada and learned how to paint after settling in Boston. He moved to Providence in 1870, and most of his best work was done there. He was one of the first commercially successful African American painters. His 1876 work *Under the Oaks* won first prize at the Philadelphia Centennial Exhibition. Another painting from that year, *Oak Trees*, is featured above. Today, his work is on display at the Rhode Island School of Design Museum, the Smithsonian American Art Museum, and other museums around the country.

? Want to know more? See www.aaa.si.edu/guides/pastguides/afriamer/bannist.htm

After the American Revolution, Gilbert Stuart of North Kingstown was one of the country's foremost painters. His portrait of President George Washington is on the dollar bill. In the late 1800s, Edward Bannister created paintings of idealized landscapes.

A WAY WITH WORDS

Some of Rhode Island's earliest leaders were notable writers, including Roger Williams. He wrote several books on religious issues and published a book on the Narragansett people and their language, *A Key into the Language of America*. The 19th-century poet Julia Ward Howe, who wrote the lyrics to "Battle Hymn of the Republic," was related to two colonial governors

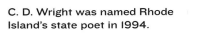
C. D. Wright was named Rhode Island's state poet in 1994.

of Rhode Island. More recently, C. D. Wright, who teaches at Brown University, has written poems with a strong Rhode Island voice. In 1994, she was named the state poet.

Children's author Avi spent many years living in Providence and set some of his books there, including *Something Upstairs: A Tale of Ghosts*. In 2003, he won the Newbery Medal—given to the best children's book of the year—for *Crispin: The Cross of Lead*. Natalie Babbitt, an award-winning children's author who lives in Providence, wrote the fantasy book *Tuck Everlasting*. Another Rhode Island author who kids—and adults—enjoying reading is David Macaulay. After studying architecture at RISD, he went on to write and illustrate books such as *The Way Things Work* and *Pyramid*.

MINI-BIO

JULIA WARD HOWE: POET OF THE REPUBLIC

Julia Ward Howe (1819–1910) devoted her life to words and helping others. She published her first work while still a teen, and she went on to write poems, plays, and essays. Howe strongly opposed slavery and called for giving women the right to vote. In 1861, while the Civil War raged, she wrote the lyrics for the song "The Battle Hymn of the Republic." She set the words to an existing tune called "John Brown's Body." The song was meant to inspire Union troops fighting against the South. The lyrics remain her best-known work.

? Want to know more? See www25.uua.org/uuhs/duub/articles/juliawardhowe.html

STAGE AND SCREEN

One of the greatest entertainers of the early 20th century hailed from Rhode Island. George M. Cohan was born in Providence to a family of traveling entertainers who soon put young George in their act. He became a singer, dancer, and producer. He also wrote songs such as "I'm a Yankee Doodle Dandy" and "Give My Regards to Broadway."

Rhode Islanders have perhaps made their biggest screen impact behind the camera. Michael Corrente of Pawtucket has directed several films that were also shot in

MINI-BIO

SISSIERETTA JOYNER JONES: SINGER SUPREME

Sissieretta Joyner Jones (1869–1933) was born in Virginia and moved to Providence as a child, where she soon impressed members of her church with her singing talents. She studied music and began her professional career in 1888. Her extraordinary voice won her many admirers, and she gave private concerts for several U.S. presidents. But as an African American, she was not allowed to sing in the world's great opera houses, despite her talents. In 1915, she returned to Rhode Island to take care of her sick mother and never sang professionally again.

Want to know more? See www.lkwdpl.org/wihohio/jone-sis.htm

THE LONGEST GAME

Pawtucket's McCoy Stadium was the site of the longest professional baseball game ever played. The game—between the Pawtucket Red Sox and the Rochester (New York) Red Wings—began at 8:00 P.M. on April 18, 1981. At 4:09 A.M. the next morning, the game was stopped with the score tied after 32 innings. The final inning was played about two months later, with the PawSox winning 3–2.

Providence, such as *Outside Providence*. For television, Seth MacFarlane created *Family Guy*, which features Peter Griffin and his wacky family. MacFarlane, who went to RISD, set the show in the made-up town of Quahog, Rhode Island.

Movies and TV shows rely on music to add to their emotional impact. Two Rhode Islanders made their careers writing music for films. Pawtucket's Wendy Carlos wrote the music for *Tron* and other movies. She was the first musician to introduce the synthesizer, a computerized keyboard, to a wide audience. Bill Conti of Providence wrote the music for most of the *Rocky* films and a number of popular TV shows.

Some Rhode Island singers have found success onstage. Opera singer Sissieretta Joyner Jones was the first African American to perform at New York's Carnegie Hall.

SPORTS

Rhode Island doesn't have any major league sports teams. Most sports fans follow the pro teams in nearby Boston, while also rooting for minor league teams such as the Pawtucket Red Sox (baseball) and the Providence Bruins (hockey).

College teams attract lots of fans. The Providence College Friars have fielded many good teams in men's basketball, and the University of Rhode Island Rams were once a basketball powerhouse. The fast break—when a player rebounds an opponent's missed shot and then quickly moves to the other end of the court to take a shot—was supposedly perfected at the University of Rhode Island under Hall of Fame coach Frank Keaney.

Rhode Island has also produced great athletes. Hall of Fame baseball player Napoleon "Nap" Lajoie was one of the greatest hitters of the early 20th century. And Ellison Myers Brown was a two-time winner of the Boston Marathon, one of the world's premier long-distance races.

In the past, Newport was a leader in American sports. The first polo match on U.S. soil took place there in 1876, as did the first open golf tournament (1895) and the National Lawn Tennis Championship (1881). Newport is also the home of the International Tennis Hall of Fame, and the city has hosted many America's Cup races, the top sailing event in the world.

MINI-BIO

ELLISON MYERS BROWN: MARATHON MAN

Ellison Myers Brown (1914–1975) was a Narragansett from Westerly. His Narragansett name was Deerfoot, but running fans knew him as Tarzan. He ran marathons, 26-mile (42 km) road races that push runners to the limit. He raced in the Boston Marathon nine times, winning twice. In 1936, he represented the United States at the Berlin Olympics. Brown was known for his great speed and endurance.

? Want to know more? See http://members.shaw.ca/tarzanbrown/

A doubles match at the International Tennis Hall of Fame in Newport

84

READ ABOUT

Child-care workers and their supporters attend a rally at the Rhode Island capitol.

CHAPTER SEVEN

GOVERNMENT

★

EACH YEAR, RHODE ISLAND HIGH SCHOOL STUDENTS TAKE PART IN THE CAPITOL FORUM. They meet at the Rhode Island State House and discuss key international issues. Then they vote on the ones that concern them most. Their views are then sent to lawmakers in Washington, D.C. In 2007, Rhode Island students said global environmental damage and the spread of weapons of mass destruction were their top worries. In programs such as this, even Rhode Islanders too young to vote are able to have their say in the government.

Rhode Island once had five state capitals—at the same time! It had one for each county.

THE CENTER OF THE GOVERNMENT

Providence is the capital of Rhode Island, and most major government officials have their offices there or in neighboring towns. The most impressive state building in the capital is the State House, which sits on Smith Hill. On its three floors, elected officials shape the state's laws. Both the legislature and the office of the governor are in the State House.

The details of Rhode Island's government are spelled out in the state constitution. The first one was written in 1843, and many amendments have been made over the years.

Capital City

This map shows places of interest in Providence, Rhode Island's capital city.

44

1

Roger Williams National Memorial

Rhode Island State Capitol

Old State House

Governor Henry Lippitt House Museum

Benefit Street's Mile of History

95

The RISD Museum

Providence Athenaeum

The Arcade

Rhode Island Black Heritage Society

Governor Stephen Hopkins House

1

44

John Brown House Museum

Bayard Ewing Building

PROVIDENCE

Providence River

195

The state capitol in Providence

Rhode Island's government, like the federal government, has three branches. The legislative branch makes laws. The executive branch carries out the laws and sometimes proposes new ones. The judicial branch makes sure the laws are carried out fairly.

THE EXECUTIVE BRANCH

The governor is the head of the executive branch. He or she either accepts or rejects proposed laws, called

Capitol Facts

Here are some fascinating facts about Rhode Island's state capitol.

Size	330 feet (101 m) long, 180 feet (55 m) wide, 233 feet (71 m) high
Year completed	1900
Dome	Fourth-largest self-supporting dome in the world
Statue on top	*Independent Man* stands 11 feet (3.4 m) tall and weighs about 500 pounds (227 kg)

Rhode Island State Government

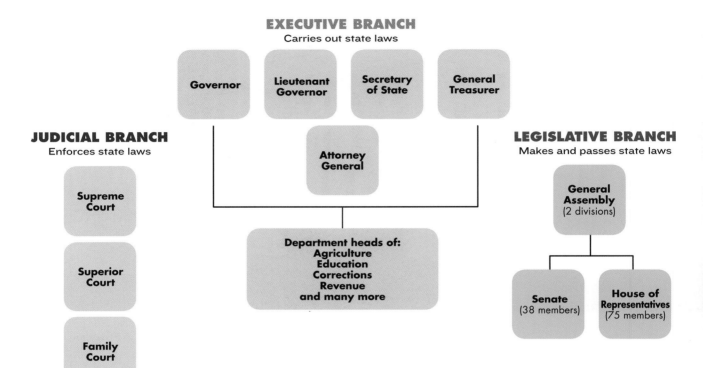

EXECUTIVE BRANCH
Carries out state laws

Governor

Lieutenant Governor

Secretary of State

General Treasurer

Attorney General

Department heads of:
Agriculture
Education
Corrections
Revenue
and many more

JUDICIAL BRANCH
Enforces state laws

Supreme Court

Superior Court

Family Court

Workers Compensation Court

Traffic Tribunal

LEGISLATIVE BRANCH
Makes and passes state laws

General Assembly
(2 divisions)

Senate
(38 members)

House of Representatives
(75 members)

bills, that have been passed by the legislature. The governor can issue executive orders, which do not have to be approved by lawmakers. One recent executive order provided help to some people who could not afford to buy medicines. The governor is responsible for proposing a state budget, but state lawmakers have the final say on how much money is spent. The governor also chooses people to lead various departments. The state senate must approve most of these choices.

Rhode Islanders also elect a lieutenant governor, who takes over if the governor can no longer serve. Day to day, the lieutenant governor works on important state issues, such as providing affordable health care and supporting small businesses.

Other executive branch officials include the secretary of state, who is in charge of running elections. The general treasurer invests the state's money, looking for the safest ways to make more of it. The attorney general makes sure the state's laws are enforced and represents Rhode Island in legal matters. In 2006, Rhode Island attorney general Patrick Lynch won the first lawsuit in the nation against companies that made lead paint, which can cause severe illnesses. As a result, the companies may have to pay up to $3.75 billion to remove the paint.

THE LEGISLATIVE BRANCH

Rhode Island's lawmakers form the General Assembly, which includes the house of representatives and the

SEE IT HERE!

OLD STATE HOUSE

The current Rhode Island State House replaced one that opened in 1762. That older building is known as the Old State House. Several historic events took place in the Old State House. On May 4, 1776, Rhode Island lawmakers broke their allegiance to Great Britain's King George III. After the American Revolution, state lawmakers met there and called for the gradual freeing of Rhode Island's slaves. Today, the building is the home of the Rhode Island Historical Preservation & Heritage Commission.

MINI-BIO

ELIZABETH ROBERTS: DEDICATED PUBLIC SERVANT

Elizabeth Roberts (1957–) first ventured to Rhode Island from her native Virginia to attend Brown University. After school, she remained in the state to work and raise a family. In 1996, she was elected to the Rhode Island Senate, and she made health care one of her major issues. Though Roberts is a Democrat, her dedication earned her the respect of Republicans. In 2006, she was elected lieutenant governor, making her the first female in Rhode Island to hold that post.

 Want to know more? See www.ltgov.ri.gov

Rhode Island Counties

This map shows the five counties in Rhode Island. Providence, the state capital, is indicated with a star.

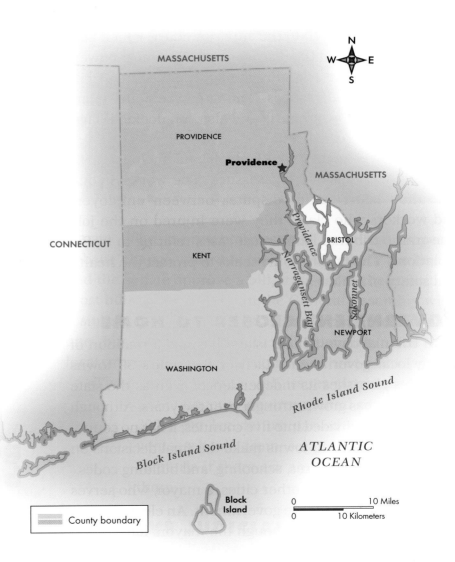

Members of the Narragansett Nation prepare for their annual meeting in Charlestown.

day operations. Some small towns also have town meetings, an old New England tradition. All town residents who attend the meeting can vote on how local taxes are spent and other important issues.

On the Narragansett lands in Charlestown, tribal members choose a chief sachem and a tribal council. These officials make business decisions for the tribes and provide essential services. Although Wampanoags and other Native Americans live in Rhode Island, the nation of Narragansetts is the only one recognized by the U.S. government. By U.S. law, each recognized tribe in the country is considered an independent nation, though its members are still U.S. citizens.

WEIRD AND WACKY LAWS

Every state has some wacky laws that are still on the books (though they're seldom—if ever—enforced), and Rhode Island is no different. Here are a few:

- In Woonsocket, don't even think about shooting icicles off of buildings with a gun.
- An old law in Foster says that if a dentist pulls the wrong tooth from a patient's mouth, the village blacksmith can pull one of the doc's teeth—or the dentist must pay a fine.
- A state law says that you can't test a horse's speed by racing it on a public highway.

State Flag

In 1897, Rhode Island became the third state to adopt an official state flag. The flag has a white background, with a golden anchor in the center. Underneath, a blue ribbon is inscribed with the word *Hope* in gold letters. Thirteen gold stars representing the original 13 states form a circle around the anchor and the ribbon.

State Seal

Rhode Island's state seal shows a golden anchor with the word *Hope* above it. A border around the anchor reads "Seal of the State of Rhode Island and Providence Plantations 1636."

READ ABOUT

A worker restores the hull of a sailboat at the International Yacht Restoration School in Newport.

CHAPTER EIGHT

ECONOMY

★

RHODE ISLAND IS SOMETIMES CALLED THE BIRTHPLACE OF THE AMERICAN INDUSTRIAL REVOLUTION, THANKS TO SAMUEL SLATER AND HIS COTTON MILL. Today, Rhode Island workers make a variety of products from jewelry to medicines to sleek yachts. Even more state residents make their living helping others—keeping them well, taking care of their money, running their governments. And state leaders hope to make Rhode Island a thriving home of new technology, to attract more workers and businesses to the state.

FROM THE LAND AND SEA

Raising crops and livestock was once an important part of the Rhode Island economy. Breeders created two animals closely associated with the state. The Rhode Island Red chicken is the state bird, and the Narragansett pacer was once the most popular racing horse in North America. But today, farming and livestock make up just a small part of the economy, and Rhode Island is

What Do Rhode Islanders Do?

This color-coded chart shows what industries Rhode Islanders work in.

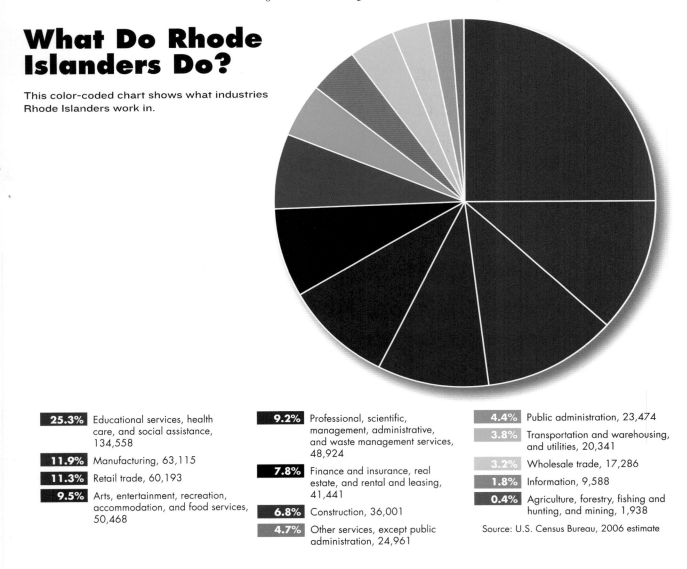

25.3% Educational services, health care, and social assistance, 134,558

11.9% Manufacturing, 63,115

11.3% Retail trade, 60,193

9.5% Arts, entertainment, recreation, accommodation, and food services, 50,468

9.2% Professional, scientific, management, administrative, and waste management services, 48,924

7.8% Finance and insurance, real estate, and rental and leasing, 41,441

6.8% Construction, 36,001

4.7% Other services, except public administration, 24,961

4.4% Public administration, 23,474

3.8% Transportation and warehousing, and utilities, 20,341

3.2% Wholesale trade, 17,286

1.8% Information, 9,588

0.4% Agriculture, forestry, fishing and hunting, and mining, 1,938

Source: U.S. Census Bureau, 2006 estimate

Rhode Island fishers haul a net into their boat.

49th out of the 50 states in the value of its crops and livestock. Most farms and orchards are in the western part of the state. The top products are plants, trees, and flowers grown by nurseries and greenhouses, followed by corn and dairy products.

Fishing is another industry that was once key for Rhode Islanders but has gone into decline. Still, some fishing fleets leave the docks of towns such as Little Compton and Galilee, and clams and oysters are farmed in saltwater ponds and near Block Island. Recreational fishers, many of them tourists, add to Rhode Island's economy. They rent or buy equipment and spend money at restaurants and hotels.

Top Products

Agriculture Greenhouse/nursery products, corn, potatoes, apples, hay, dairy products, cattle, chickens, eggs
Manufacturing Electrical equipment, appliances, and components; jewelry; computer and electronic products; textiles
Mining Sand and gravel

Major Agricultural and Mining Products

This map shows where Rhode Island's major agricultural and mining products come from. See a milk carton? That means dairy is found there.

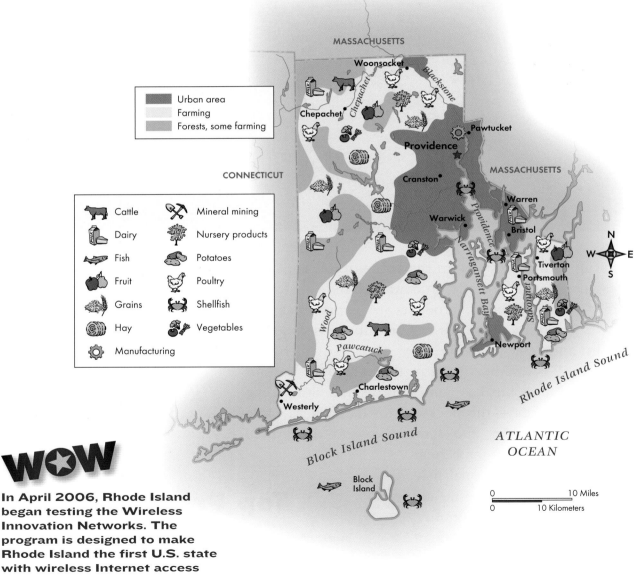

Urban area
Farming
Forests, some farming

Cattle
Dairy
Fish
Fruit
Grains
Hay
Manufacturing

Mineral mining
Nursery products
Potatoes
Poultry
Shellfish
Vegetables

WOW

In April 2006, Rhode Island began testing the Wireless Innovation Networks. The program is designed to make Rhode Island the first U.S. state with wireless Internet access available to all its residents.

MAKING GOODS

Manufacturing is in decline across New England. Many mills and factories have been torn down or turned into office space, housing, or stores. But some 63,000 Rhode Islanders still work in manufacturing. Rhode Island is a world leader in producing inexpensive jewelry, and some textiles are still made in the state. Rhode Island's top manufactured products are all kinds of electrical equipment and parts. Electric Boat, a company in Quonset Point, builds submarines for the U.S. Navy.

Some Rhode Island manufacturers are devoted to making life more fun. The state is home to several yacht and sailboat builders, including Vanguard and Goetz Marine Technology. And the headquarters for Hasbro, maker of Monopoly and Fisher-Price toys, is in Pawtucket.

High-tech industries have been growing in Rhode Island. Companies such as Tellart design new ways to use computers, while other companies build parts that are used with computers. American Power Conversion of West Kingston sells more than $2 billion worth of backup power sources for computers.

MINI-BIO

HENRY HASSENFELD: TOY MAN

A Jewish immigrant from Poland, Henry Hassenfeld (?–1960) began his business empire in 1923, selling textile scraps. With his brother Helal, he founded Hassenfeld Brothers. The company, which later became Hasbro, soon began making school supplies and, finally, toys. Henry and his sons Merrill and Harold were running the company when they introduced the first toy ever advertised on television: Mr. Potato Head. Hasbro became one of the largest toy companies in the world. Some of its popular products are Transformers, G.I. Joe, and Monopoly. Henry Hassenfeld's family still plays a role in running the company.

? Want to know more? See www.hasbro.com/default.cfm?page=ci_history_hasbro

SEE IT HERE!

VANGUARD SAILBOATS

The smell of salt is in the air at the Vanguard boatyard in Portsmouth. Vanguard, the maker of Sunfish and other sailboats, offers an hour-long tour that shows the entire boatbuilding process. Rhode Island's early boat makers used wood, but Vanguard's vessels are made from fiberglass and other strong but light materials. If you plan to stop in and say "Ahoy," contact Vanguard first to arrange your tour.

MINI-BIO

MATT COTTAM: DESIGN WIZARD

After graduating from the Rhode Island School of Design, Matt Cottam (1973–) stayed in Providence and cofounded his own design business. His company, Tellart, makes sensors that can detect heat, motion, sound, or light and then use that energy to control motors or send information to a Web site. He has also worked with Brown University students to design a new kind of suit worn by people who handle hazardous materials such as deadly chemicals. With the new suit, a person can get dressed alone, rather than needing help, as with the old suits. Cottam's suits also offer more protection. His design work highlights the new, creative thinking going on in Rhode Island industry.

? Want to know more? See www.tellart.com/media/gallery_ppl_cu.php

WORD TO KNOW

genetic engineering *changing genes, the chemicals in plants and animals that determine the traits passed from one generation to the next*

Some companies in Rhode Island are using **genetic engineering** to make new medicines. In 2005, Amgen opened a plant in West Greenwich that runs 24 hours a day, seven days a week, making a drug to treat arthritis. In 2006, another high-tech drug maker, Alexion, bought a plant in Smithfield, where it will make new medicines. A law passed in 2006 lowered taxes for companies that use genetic engineering to make products so more of them would be tempted to come to Rhode Island.

SERVICES OF ALL KINDS

When you go to the bank, buy a burger, or take your bike in for repairs, you're using the services of some company. In Rhode Island, service industries dominate the economy. Service industries help people invest their money, provide health care, teach children, and sell goods. Woonsocket is the home of one of the country's top drugstores, CVS Caremark. The company has 6,200 stores across the country.

The state's media—newspapers, TV and radio stations, and Web sites—help keep Rhode Islanders informed about events in the state, across the country, and around the world. The state's largest newspaper is the *Providence Journal*, and several other cities, includ-

Hotel clerks are among the many service workers who contribute to Rhode Island's economy.

ing Woonsocket and Pawtucket, also have daily papers. Rhode Island has six television stations. Many viewers also watch channels out of Boston.

Everyone loves a good vacation, and Rhode Islanders are no different. They, along with visitors from other states, spend almost $5 billion every year on tourism. Tourism is the state's fastest-growing industry. Tourists are attracted to the state's beaches, waters, and historic sites.

THE CAPITAL REGION

THINGS TO DO: Shop in America's oldest mall, see the country's first mill, and get a good look at an anteater.

Providence

★ **First Baptist Church:** In 1638, Roger Williams started the first Baptist church in North America. By the 1770s, the members decided they needed a new home, and they built this grand church. The church features beautiful carved wood, a crystal chandelier, and a 185-foot-tall (56 m) steeple.

★ **Roger Williams Park Zoo:** This zoo is Rhode Island's top outdoor tourist attraction and one of the oldest zoos in the United States. It has elephants, giraffes, polar bears, anteaters, and many more creatures.

Polar bears at the Roger Williams Park Zoo

SEE IT HERE!

BIG BLUE BUG

Driving on Interstate 95 in Providence, it's hard to miss the Big Blue Bug. The steel, wire-mesh, and fiberglass termite weighs in at 2 tons and is 58 feet (18 m) long. The giant termite, which was named Nibbles Woodaway in a contest, was erected in 1980 to advertise a pest-control business. Since then, it has been featured in many movies and TV shows. Each Christmas, it's dressed up with a Santa beard.

Italian ice cream called gelato

★ **Federal Hill:** Getting hungry for some pasta, pizza, or creamy Italian ice cream? Then Federal Hill is the place to go. Almost 50 restaurants are packed into the neighborhood, which has been populated by Italian Americans for more than 100 years. In recent years, Mexican and Indian restaurants have added to the area's eating delights.

Visitors at the Rhode Island School of Design Museum

★ **Rhode Island School of Design Museum:** Stand beneath a towering but serene Asian statue, or immerse yourself in a painting of a misty landscape. Don't like those? Then keep moving, because there's a lot more to see at the school's art museum. Its collection includes more than 80,000 pieces.

★ **Rhode Island Black Heritage Society Museum:** African Americans played a huge part in Rhode Island's history. This museum tells the story of the state's African Americans in colonial and modern times.

★ **The Arcade:** When the Arcade opened in 1828, it was the first indoor shopping mall in the United States. Shoppers still come to the Arcade for a bargain—and to see a little bit of history.

★ **American Diner Museum:** This museum contains company records, drawings, promotional brochures, and equipment from several diner manufacturing companies along with a few diner cars.

★ **Providence Children's Museum:** If you want to explore the whats and whys of water, this museum is the place for you. There are also exhibits on subjects ranging from the human body to the settlers of Rhode Island.

★ **Juan Pablo Duarte Statue:** Dominicans are the second-largest Hispanic group in Rhode Island, and this statue honors Duarte, a founder of the Dominican Republic.

East Providence

★ **Crescent Park Carousel:** Here the music still plays and the horses still whirl. Opened in 1895, the ride was designed by Charles I. D. Looff, a master carousel maker who immigrated from Denmark. His creation in East Providence has 66 hand-carved horses, and the tails are made from real horsehair!

Carousel pony at
Crescent Park

Pawtucket

★ **Slater Mill:** Samuel Slater opened the nation's first mechanized textile mill on this site in 1793. Today, that building and the water-wheel that powered his machines still stand. Another mill building from 1810 features working textile machines.

Cranston

★ **Sprague Mansion:** Governor William Sprague came from one of America's wealthiest families, and his family's 28-room mansion was the site of large, fancy parties. Sprague eventually lost most of his fortune and had to sell the home. Today, ghosts of his father and several others are said to haunt the house. Visit it—if you dare!

NORTHERN RHODE ISLAND

THINGS TO DO: Explore the Blackstone River, see the silliness at the Ancient and Horribles Parade, and have some quiet time outdoors at a nature refuge.

Woonsocket

★ **Museum of Work and Culture:** This museum follows the journey of French Canadians who left their homes in Canada to work in the mills of Rhode Island.
★ **Blackstone River Rapids:** The Blackstone River cuts through northeastern Rhode Island, and its waters have powered many of the state's mills. Today, thrill seekers rush over its rapids in canoes and kayaks.

The tour boat *Samuel Slater* on the Blackstone River

Chepachet

★ **Ancient and Horribles Parade:**
If you want a traditional Fourth of
July parade with marching bands,
don't come to Chepachet. The
annual parade here is more about
poking fun at people and events
than celebrating the nation's
birthday. Since 1927, locals have
donned strange costumes and
made wacky floats, but traditional
marching bands and fire trucks
take part, too.

Smithfield

★ **Powder Mill Ledges Wildlife
Refuge:** The trails of this wildlife
refuge will take you past animals
and wildflowers. The site also
offers workshops on natural life in
Rhode Island.

WESTERN RHODE ISLAND AND WEST BAY

**THINGS TO DO: Explore the shoreline near
Conimicut Point Lighthouse, gaze at the sky at
the Seagrave Memorial Observatory, and learn
about steam engines and their role in Rhode
Island's past.**

Conimicut Point Park

Warwick

★ **Conimicut Point Park:** This
park on Narragansett Bay offers a
beach, a playground, fishing, and
great views of the water and of
Conimicut Point Lighthouse. Built
in 1883, the lighthouse was one
of the last in the nation to use gas
rather than electricity to power its
beam.

Scituate

★ **Seagrave Memorial Observatory:**
If you want stars in your eyes,
this is the place for you. Frank
Seagrave, whose hobby was studying the night sky, built the observatory in 1914. Today, a private group
owns the building and its four
telescopes, but anyone can come
use them on a Saturday night.

East Greenwich

★ **New England Wireless and Steam Museum:** This little museum covers some big subjects—wireless communications and steam engines. The wireless room features telegraph equipment and some of the first radios. The collection of working steam engines includes one from Rhode Island's Corliss Steam Engine Company, as well as other local manufacturers.

THE EAST BAY

THINGS TO DO: Stroll the historic docks of Warren, bike along the shore, and enjoy the same view Metacomet once had of his Wampanoag lands.

Warren

★ **Warren Street Docks:** This historic neighborhood in one of Rhode Island's oldest towns has buildings dating back to the American Revolution.

In 1785, Bristol celebrated the Fourth of July with a parade, and it has held one ever since, making it the oldest Independence Day celebration in the country.

Tapping maple trees at the Coggeshall Farm Museum

Bristol

★ **Coggeshall Farm Museum:** Wonder what life was like on a Rhode Island farm more than 200 years ago? The Coggeshall Farm Museum lets you see for yourself. Actors dressed in 18th-century clothes do the same tasks that farmers did in the 1790s. They press apples into cider and tap maple trees for their sap, which is turned into syrup.

★ **Colt State Park:** This park offers a tremendous view of Narragansett Bay. Bike trails wind along the bay and through fruit trees. There's also a dock, a fishing pier, and picnic grounds.

* **Herreshoff Marine Museum:** Yachting has a long history in Rhode Island, and the Herreshoff Manufacturing Company made some of the world's fastest sailing boats. Now the company's former plant is the site of the Herreshoff Marine Museum, which features Herreshoff yachts up to 100 years old.
* **Haffenreffer Museum of Anthropology:** This museum is part of Brown University. It was built on land that served as the home of Metacomet (King Philip), the Wampanoag sachem. On the museum's grounds is a granite "seat" called King Philip's Throne. From there, Metacomet could look out over his people's lands and the nearby waters. Inside the museum are collections featuring items from Native groups across North and South America, as well as Africa and Australia.

Prudence Island

* **Heritage Foundation of Rhode Island Park:** Prudence Island, which is a short ferry ride from Bristol, is home to only about 150 families. Most of the island is undeveloped. The park has great hiking trails that offer views of birds and the surrounding bay.

NEWPORT COUNTY

THINGS TO DO: Explore the grand mansions of Newport, poke around in Gray's Store, the oldest general store in the country, and see a green elephant in Portsmouth.

Newport

* **Naval War College Museum:** This museum delves into U.S. naval history, especially events that took place in Narragansett Bay. No need to salute!
* **Cliff Walk:** For the perfect view of the water and the Newport "cottages" that line it, take a stroll along the Cliff Walk, a 3.5-mile (5.6 km) trail that runs between the houses and the sea. Along the way, you'll see magnificent mansions such as the Breakers and Rosecliff.

Mansions along Cliff Walk

★ **God's Little Acre Burial Ground:** This cemetery, which has graves dating to 1718, is the burial site of many of Newport's enslaved Africans and free blacks.

★ **New England Aquarium Exploration Center:** Want to get up close and personal with sea stars or hermit crabs? Then head to the "touch tank" at the Exploration Center, where you can pet some of the sea creatures.

★ **Rose Island Lighthouse:** The lighthouse on Rose Island, which lies more than 1 mile (1.6 km) offshore, was built in 1870. Most visitors explore the island and the lighthouse during the day. The people who rent rooms in the lighthouse and stay the night help run the lights.

Rose Island Lighthouse

SEE IT HERE!

FORT ADAMS

After the War of 1812, Americans wanted more protection from future naval attacks. Fort Adams was constructed in Newport between 1824 and 1857, and it became the largest coastal fort in the United States. The fort was built to hold more than 400 guns, though fewer were actually installed. The fort ceased serving as a military base in the 1950s and is now part of a state park. Each year, two popular music festivals, one for jazz and one for folk, are held just outside Fort Adams's thick stone walls. The grounds around the fort feature ball fields, beaches, and a boat ramp.

★ **Newport Casino:** There's no gambling at this historic casino, which was built in 1880 as a sports club. Today, it's the home of the International Tennis Hall of Fame and a tennis museum. Sports such as tennis and croquet are still played there, too.

SUPPORTER OF HIS FAITH

Jewish settlers had first reached Rhode Island some 100 years before Aaron Lopez (1731–1782) arrived, but it was Lopez who helped build one of the first synagogues in North America. His family had lived in Portugal before immigrating. They settled in Newport, where they made a fortune producing candles and soap before branching out into shipbuilding and the slave trade. In the early 1760s, Aaron Lopez put up money to build Touro Synagogue. During the American Revolution, Lopez used his business skills to help supply U.S. troops.

★ **Touro Synagogue:** In 1763, the Jewish community in Newport opened one of the first synagogues in the United States. Peter Harrison, a noted colonial architect, designed the building. Today, Touro Synagogue is still used for religious services.

Inside Touro Synagogue

Tiverton

★ **Newport Butterfly Farm:** All kinds of butterflies are raised at this farm, which also features a "zoo" filled with the beautiful insects. On sunny days, visitors can stroll through the greenhouse where the butterflies fly, eat, and lay eggs.

Middletown

★ **Purgatory Chasm:** Above Second Beach is a rocky cliff with a giant chasm, or split, in the rocks. Folk legends say the devil hit the rocks with an ax, resulting in this 160-foot-deep (49 m) chasm. Actually, the movement of glaciers millions of years ago created the split, and more recent sea erosion has added to it. You can cross Purgatory Chasm on a small wooden bridge and see the sea below.

Green Animals Topiary Garden

Portsmouth

★ **Green Animals Topiary Garden:**
Ever seen a green elephant? You
will, at the Green Animals Topiary
Garden. A huge elephant and 20
other creatures have been shaped
out of bushes and hedges. The
garden, the oldest of its kind in
the United States, also has bushy,
living sculptures of geometric
shapes and fancy designs.

Jamestown

★ **Beavertail Lighthouse Museum:**
To shed some light on the history
of Rhode Island lighthouses, check
out this museum. It's housed next
to the third-oldest U.S. lighthouse,
which was built in 1749. The
museum also has an exhibit on the
lives of lighthouse keepers.

SEE IT HERE!

GRAY'S STORE

General stores are a New England tradition. Before
there were modern department stores, farmers and
others bought their goods here. Gray's Store in Little
Compton first opened its doors in 1788 and claims to
be the oldest continually run general store in the nation.
Inside is a post office that opened in 1804 and an
old-time soda fountain. Stop by for candy, clothing, or
cornmeal to make johnnycakes.

Little Compton

★ **Rhode Island Red Plaque:**
Adamsville, a village within Little
Compton, was the birthplace of
the first Rhode Island Red chicken,
which is now the official state bird.
A plaque mounted on a granite
stone marks the occasion. The Reds
are prized for
both their eggs
and their meat.

Rhode Island Red chicken

FAQ ★ ★ ★

Q8 WHAT IS SOUTH COUNTY?

A8 South County isn't really a county at all. It's just a nickname for the towns that form Washington County.

SOUTH COUNTY

THINGS TO DO: Hit the beach at Misquamicut, stroll through the streets of Watch Hill, and enjoy the dancing at a powwow.

North Kingstown

★ **Quonset Air Museum:** The museum building was once part of the Quonset Point Naval Air Station. Now it traces the role Rhode Island played in U.S. aviation history. On display are military airplanes and helicopters, some dating back to World War II.

Westerly

★ **Misquamicut State Beach:** Looking for fun in the sun? Join beachgoers from across southern New England at Misquamicut. Along the beach are clam shacks and ice cream shops, an amusement park, and waterslides.

★ **Watch Hill:** This village got its name during the American Revolution, when local residents stood watch for attacking British ships. Today, it boasts quaint shops, a lighthouse, and great beaches.

New Shoreham

★ **North Light:** Older lighthouses on Block Island were made from wood. The building at North Light is made of granite and iron, so it can withstand almost any storm. The tower is not open to the public, but the lighthouse's first floor has a small museum.

Charlestown

★ **Narragansett Indian Powwows:** On their tribal lands and at other sites, Narragansetts hold several powwows each year. People come from far and wide to enjoy the singing, dancing, and food.

Dancer at a Narragansett powwow

WRITING PROJECTS

Check out these ideas for creating a campaign brochure and writing you-are-there narratives. Or act out interviews with famous people from the state.

118

ART PROJECTS

You can illustrate the state song, create a dazzling PowerPoint presentation, or learn about the state quarter and design your own.

119

TIMELINE

What happened when? This timeline highlights important events in the state's history—and shows what was happening throughout the United States at the same time.

122

FAST FACTS

Use this section to find fascinating facts about state symbols, land area and population statistics, weather, sports teams, and much more.

126

GLOSSARY

Remember the Words to Know from the chapters in this book? They're all collected here.

125

SCIENCE, TECHNOLOGY, & MATH PROJECTS

Make weather maps, graph population statistics, and research endangered species that live in the state.

120

PRIMARY VS. SECONDARY SOURCES

121

So what are primary and secondary sources? And what's the diff? This section explains all that and where you can find them.

BIOGRAPHICAL DICTIONARY

133

This at-a-glance guide highlights some of the state's most important and influential people. Visit this section and read about their contributions to the state, the country, and the world.

RESOURCES

Books, Web sites, DVDs, and more. Take a look at these additional sources for information about the state.

137

WRITING PROJECTS

★ ★ ★

Write a Memoir, Journal, or Editorial for Your School Newspaper!

Picture Yourself . . .

★ Building a Narragansett wigwam. You'll need sticks, animal skins, tree bark, and long leaves. Describe how you will put them together.

SEE: Chapter Two, pages 24–25.
GO TO: http://oldsturbridgevillage.org/explore_learn/document_viewer.php?Action=View&DocID=2072&PF=Y

★ Taking part in the Dorr Rebellion. Write an editorial for your school newspaper explaining why you believe Rhode Island's voting requirements are unfair and how you want them changed.

SEE: Chapter Four, pages 54–55.
GO TO: www.dorrrebellionmuseum.org

Create an Election Brochure or Web Site!

Run for office! Throughout this book, you've read about some of the issues that concern Rhode Island today. As a candidate for governor of Rhode Island, create a campaign brochure or Web site.

★ Explain how you meet the qualifications to be governor of Rhode Island.

★ Talk about the three or four major issues you'll focus on if you're elected.

★ Remember, you'll be responsible for Rhode Island's budget. How would you spend the taxpayers' money?

SEE: Chapter Seven, pages 87–89.

GO TO: Rhode Island's government Web site at www.ri.gov. You might also want to read some local newspapers. Try these:

Providence Journal: www.projo.com

Newport Daily News: www.newportdailynews.com

Create an interview script with a famous person from Rhode Island!

★ Research various famous Rhode Islanders, such as Roger Williams, Bill Conti, David Macaulay, Sissieretta Joyner Jones, Ruth Simmons, Seth MacFarlane, Ellison Myers Brown, and many others.

★ Based on your research, pick one person you would most like to interview.

★ Write a script of the interview. What questions would you ask? How would this famous person answer? Create a question-and-answer format. You may want to supplement this writing project with a voice-recording dramatization of the interview.

SEE: Chapter Three, pages 33–39, Chapter Six, pages 78–83, and the Biographical Dictionary, pages 133–136.

GO TO: www.quahog.org/factsfolklore/index.php?id=7

ART PROJECTS

★ ★ ★

Create a PowerPoint Presentation or Visitors' Guide
Welcome to Rhode Island!

Rhode Island is a great place to visit and to live! From its natural beauty to its bustling cities and historical sites, there's plenty to see and do. In your PowerPoint presentation or brochure, highlight 10 to 15 of Rhode Island's amazing landmarks. Be sure to include:

★ a map of the state showing where these sites are located

★ photos, illustrations, Web links, natural history facts, geographic stats, climate and weather info, and descriptions of plants and wildlife

SEE: Chapter Nine, pages 104–115, and Fast Facts, pages 126–127.

GO TO: The official tourism Web site for Rhode Island at www.visitrhodeisland.com. Download and print maps, photos, and vacation ideas for tourists.

Illustrate the Lyrics to the Rhode Island State Song
("Rhode Island It's For Me")

Use markers, paints, photos, collages, colored pencils, or computer graphics to illustrate the lyrics to "Rhode Island It's for Me." Turn your illustrations into a picture book, or scan them into PowerPoint and add music.

SEE: The lyrics to "Rhode Island It's for Me" on page 128.

GO TO: The Rhode Island state government Web site at www.ri.gov to find out more about the origin of the state song.

Research Rhode Island's State Quarter

From 1999 to 2008, the U.S. Mint introduced new quarters commemorating each of the 50 states in the order that they were admitted to the Union. Each state's quarter features a unique design on its back, or reverse.

★ Research the significance of the image. Who designed the quarter? Who chose the final design?

★ Design your own Rhode Island quarter. What images would you choose for the reverse?

★ Make a poster showing the Rhode Island quarter and label each image.

GO TO: www.usmint.gov/kids and find out what's featured on the back of the Rhode Island quarter.

SCIENCE, TECHNOLOGY, & MATH PROJECTS

★ ★ ★

Graph Population Statistics!

★ Compare population statistics (such as ethnic background, birth, death, and literacy rates) in Rhode Island counties or major cities.

★ In your graph or chart, look at population density and write sentences describing what the population statistics show; graph one set of population statistics and write a paragraph explaining what the graphs reveal.

SEE: Chapter Six, pages 72–75.

GO TO: The official Web site for the U.S. Census Bureau at www.census.gov and at http:// quickfacts.census.gov/qfd/states/44000.html, to find out more about population statistics, how they work, and what the statistics are for Rhode Island.

Create a Weather Map of Rhode Island!

Use your knowledge of Rhode Island's geography to research and identify conditions that result in specific weather events. What is it about the geography of Rhode Island that makes it vulnerable to things like nor'easters? Create a weather map or poster that shows the weather patterns over the state. Include a caption explaining the technology used to measure weather phenomena and provide data.

SEE: Chapter One, pages 13–14.

GO TO: The National Oceanic and Atmospheric Administration's National Weather Service Web site at www.weather.gov for weather maps and forecasts for Rhode Island.

Track Endangered Species

Using your knowledge of Rhode Island's wildlife, research which animals and plants are endangered or threatened.

★ Find out what the state is doing to protect these species.

★ Chart known populations of the animals and plants, and report on changes in certain geographic areas

SEE: Chapter One, page 17.

GO TO: Web sites such as http://ecos.fws.gov/ tess_public/StateListingAndOccurrence.do?state=RI for lists of endangered species in Rhode Island.

Leatherback turtle

PRIMARY VS. SECONDARY SOURCES

★ ★ ★

What's the Diff?

Your teacher may require at least one or two primary sources and one or two secondary sources for your assignment. So, what's the difference between the two?

★ **Primary sources are original.** You are reading the actual words of someone's diary, journal, letter, autobiography, or interview. Primary sources can also be photographs, maps, prints, cartoons, news/film footage, posters, first-person newspaper articles, drawings, musical scores, and recordings. By the way, when you conduct a survey, interview someone, shoot a video, or take photographs to include in a project, you are creating primary sources!

★ **Secondary sources are what you find in encyclopedias, textbooks, articles, biographies, and almanacs.** These are written by a person or group of people who tell about something that happened to someone else. Secondary sources also recount what another person said or did. This book is an example of a secondary source.

Now that you know what primary sources are—where can you find them?

★ **Your school or local library:** Check the library catalog for collections of original writings, government documents, musical scores, and so on. Some of this material may be stored on microfilm. The Library of Congress Web site (www.loc.gov) is an excellent online resource for primary source materials.

★ **Historical societies:** These organizations keep historical documents, photographs, and other materials. Staff members can help you find what you are looking for. History museums are also great places to see primary sources firsthand.

★ **The Internet:** There are lots of sites that have primary sources you can download and use in a project or assignment.

TIMELINE

★ ★ ★

U.S. Events | 8000 BCE | **Rhode Island Events**

c. 8000 BCE
The first humans come to Rhode Island.

500 BCE **c. 500 BCE**
The earliest known year-round village
is established on Block Island.

1200 CE **c. 1200 CE**
Algonquians begin to raise corn.
1400

1492
Christopher Columbus and his crew
sight land in the Caribbean Sea.

1500 **1500**
Narragansetts are the dominant people
in what is now Rhode Island.

1524
Giovanni da Verrazzano becomes the first
1600 European known to reach Rhode Island.

1607
The first permanent English settlement in
North America is established at Jamestown.

1620
Pilgrims found Plymouth Colony, the
second permanent English settlement.

1636
Roger Williams settles in Providence.

1638
Anne Hutchinson and her followers found Portsmouth.

1639
William Coddington founds Newport.

1643
Roger Williams receives a charter from Parliament.

1663
Rhode Island gets a new charter from King Charles II.

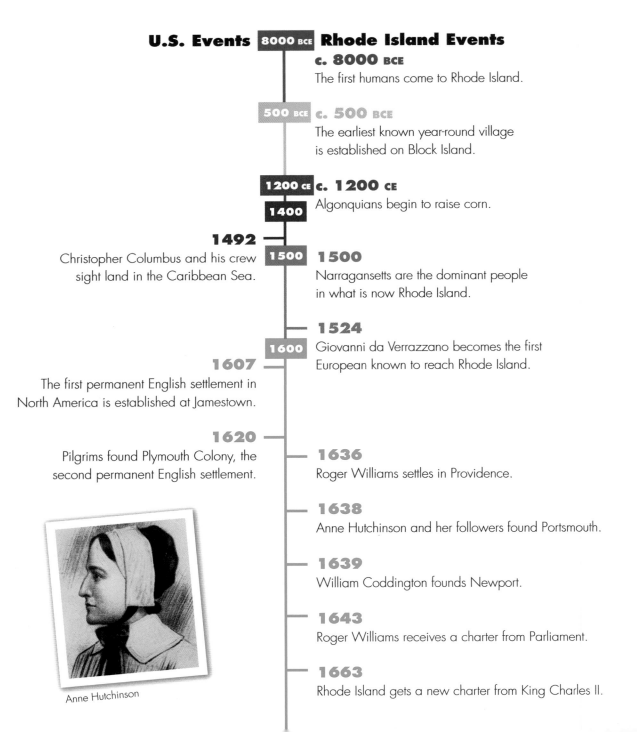

Anne Hutchinson

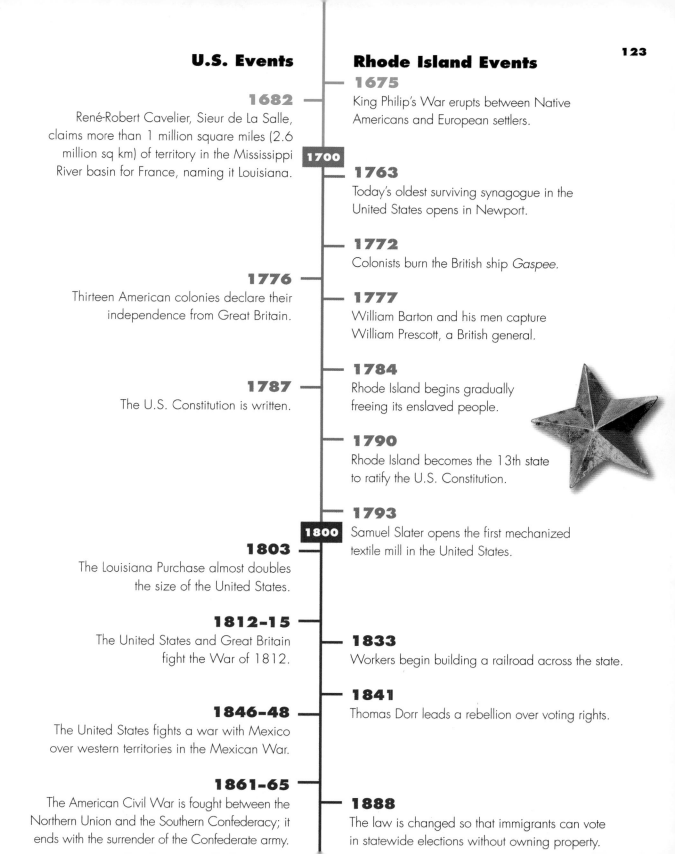

U.S. Events

1682
René-Robert Cavelier, Sieur de La Salle, claims more than 1 million square miles (2.6 million sq km) of territory in the Mississippi River basin for France, naming it Louisiana.

1776
Thirteen American colonies declare their independence from Great Britain.

1787
The U.S. Constitution is written.

1803
The Louisiana Purchase almost doubles the size of the United States.

1812–15
The United States and Great Britain fight the War of 1812.

1846–48
The United States fights a war with Mexico over western territories in the Mexican War.

1861–65
The American Civil War is fought between the Northern Union and the Southern Confederacy; it ends with the surrender of the Confederate army.

Rhode Island Events

1675
King Philip's War erupts between Native Americans and European settlers.

1700

1763
Today's oldest surviving synagogue in the United States opens in Newport.

1772
Colonists burn the British ship *Gaspee*.

1777
William Barton and his men capture William Prescott, a British general.

1784
Rhode Island begins gradually freeing its enslaved people.

1790
Rhode Island becomes the 13th state to ratify the U.S. Constitution.

1793
Samuel Slater opens the first mechanized textile mill in the United States.

1800

1833
Workers begin building a railroad across the state.

1841
Thomas Dorr leads a rebellion over voting rights.

1888
The law is changed so that immigrants can vote in statewide elections without owning property.

| U.S. Events | **1900** | Rhode Island Events |

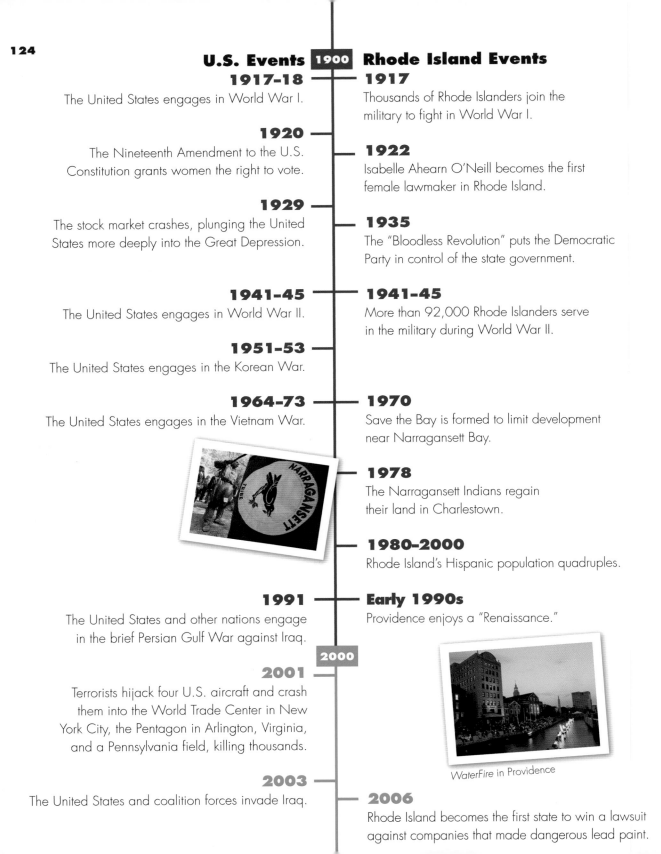

1917-18
The United States engages in World War I.

1917
Thousands of Rhode Islanders join the military to fight in World War I.

1920
The Nineteenth Amendment to the U.S. Constitution grants women the right to vote.

1922
Isabelle Ahearn O'Neill becomes the first female lawmaker in Rhode Island.

1929
The stock market crashes, plunging the United States more deeply into the Great Depression.

1935
The "Bloodless Revolution" puts the Democratic Party in control of the state government.

1941-45
The United States engages in World War II.

1941-45
More than 92,000 Rhode Islanders serve in the military during World War II.

1951-53
The United States engages in the Korean War.

1964-73
The United States engages in the Vietnam War.

1970
Save the Bay is formed to limit development near Narragansett Bay.

1978
The Narragansett Indians regain their land in Charlestown.

1980-2000
Rhode Island's Hispanic population quadruples.

1991
The United States and other nations engage in the brief Persian Gulf War against Iraq.

Early 1990s
Providence enjoys a "Renaissance."

2000

WaterFire in Providence

2001
Terrorists hijack four U.S. aircraft and crash them into the World Trade Center in New York City, the Pentagon in Arlington, Virginia, and a Pennsylvania field, killing thousands.

2003
The United States and coalition forces invade Iraq.

2006
Rhode Island becomes the first state to win a lawsuit against companies that made dangerous lead paint.

GLOSSARY

★ ★ ★

allies people who are on the same side in a conflict

appeals legal proceedings in which a court is asked to change the decision of a lower court

archaeologists people who study the remains of past human societies

artifacts items created by humans, usually for a practical purpose

banished sent out of a place forever

charter a document from a ruler granting rights to a group

colonies communities settled in a new land but with ties to another government

Constitution the written document that contains all the governing principles of the United States

corruption illegal or unfair acts committed by government or business officials

endangered in danger of becoming extinct

federal relating to the national government

genetic engineering changing genes, the chemicals in plants and animals that determine the traits passed from one generation to the next

glaciers slow-moving masses of ice

integrated brought together all members of society

Parliament the legislature in Great Britain

patriots Americans who supported independence from Great Britain

plantation a large farm that grows mainly one crop

prejudice an unreasonable hatred or fear of others

privateers private citizens given government approval to capture enemy ships

reservoir an artificial lake or tank for storing water

rogue a dishonest or worthless person

smuggle to bring in or take out illegally

strike an organized refusal to work, usually as a sign of protest about working conditions

FAST FACTS

★   ★   ★

State Symbols

Statehood date	May 29, 1790, the 13th state
Official state name	State of Rhode Island and Providence Plantations
Origin of state name	Named after the island of Rhodes in the Mediterranean Sea by explorer Giovanni da Verrazzano
State capital	Providence
State nickname	Little Rhody, the Ocean State
State motto	Hope
State bird	Rhode Island Red chicken
State flower	Violet
State rock	Cumberlandite
State mineral	Bowenite
State shell	Quahog
State song	"Rhode Island It's for Me"
State tree	Red maple
State fair	Richmond, mid-August

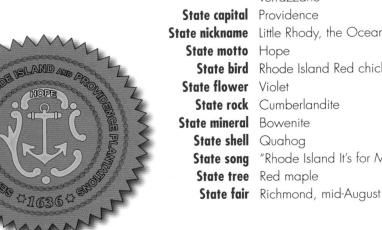

State seal

Geography

Total area; rank	1,545 square miles (4,002 sq km); 50th
Land; rank	1,045 square miles (2,707 sq km); 50th
Water; rank	500 square miles (1,295 sq km); 41st
Inland water; rank	178 square miles (461 sq km); 46th
Coastal water; rank	9 square miles (23 sq km); 20th
Territorial water; rank	314 square miles (813 sq km); 17th
Geographic center	Kent, 1 mile (1.6 km) southwest of Crompton
Latitude	41°09' N to 42°01' N
Longitude	71°07' W to 71°53' W
Highest point	Jerimoth Hill, 812 feet (247 m) above sea level
Lowest point	Sea level along the Atlantic Ocean
Largest city	Providence
Longest river	Blackstone
Counties	5

Population

Population; rank (2007 estimate)	1,057,832; 43rd
Density (2007 estimate)	1,012 persons per square miles (391 per sq km)
Population distribution (2000 census)	91% urban, 9% rural
Ethnic distribution (2007 estimate)	White persons: 88.6%[†]
	Black persons: 6.3%[†]
	Asian persons: 2.7%[†]
	American Indian and Alaska Native persons: 0.6%[†]
	Native Hawaiian and Other Pacific Islanders: 0.1%[†]
	Persons reporting two or more races: 1.5%
	Persons of Hispanic or Latino origin: 11.2%[*]
	White persons not Hispanic: 79.3%

[†] *Includes persons reporting only one race.*
[*] *Hispanics may be of any race, so they are also included in applicable race categories.*

Weather

Record high temperature	104°F (40°C) at Providence on August 2, 1975
Record low temperature	−25°F (−32°C) at Greene on February 5, 1996
Average July temperature	73°F (23°C)
Average January temperature	29°F (−2°C)
Average yearly precipitation	46 inches (117 cm)

State flag

SPORTS TEAMS

★   ★   ★

NCAA Teams (Division I)

Brown University *Bears*
Providence College *Friars*
University of Rhode Island *Rams*

The University of Rhode Island Rams in action against Nebraska's Creighton University

CULTURAL INSTITUTIONS

★ ★ ★

Libraries

The *Providence Public Library* has many specialized collections, including the Littman Art Collection and the Rhode Island Collection.

The *Rhode Island State Archives* contains materials on the state's history, including documents dating back to 1638 and thousands of photographs.

University Library, at the University of Rhode Island in Kingston, has a special collections department, which contains many rare books and manuscripts along with a collection of interviews on local history.

The *Rhode Island Historical Society Library* in Providence has the state's most significant archive for local history.

Museums

The *Museum of Natural History* (Providence) has a fantastic collection of insects, birds, and fossils, along with an exhibit on geology. Cormack Planetarium, part of the museum, has a telescope for viewing the moon, day or night.

The *Museum of Newport History* (Newport) includes ceramics, drawings, needlework, and paintings pertaining to the history of the area. Musical instruments are also on display.

The *Rhode Island Black Heritage Society Museum* (Providence) has information on the history of African Americans in Rhode Island, including photographs, paintings, documents, manuscripts, and letters.

The *Rhode Island School of Design Museum* (Providence) holds more than 80,000 pieces of art, ranging from impressionist paintings to Chinese sculpture. It also has an Egyptian gallery with an actual coffin and mummy.

Performing Arts

Rhode Island has one major symphony orchestra and one major professional theater company.

Universities and Colleges

In 2006, Rhode Island had three public and nine private institutions of higher learning.

Wendy Carlos (1939–), a native of Pawtucket, is a composer who was a pioneer in the use of synthesizers. She wrote the music for *Tron* and other films.

Elizabeth Buffum Chace See page 57.

Vincent "Buddy" Cianci (1941–) was the longtime mayor of Providence. He was loved for helping rebuild Providence but faced frequent legal problems. He was sent to prison twice, once for assault and once for corruption.

William Coddington (1601–1678) was a supporter of Anne Hutchinson and founded Newport. He later served as governor of the colony.

Bill Conti (1942–) is a composer and conductor. The Providence native has written the music for many films, including the *Rocky* movies.

George Corliss (1817–1888) was a New York native who started a business in Providence making steam engines. He made improvements to existing engines and built some of the most powerful ones of the day.

Jill Craybas

Michael Corrente (1959–) is a film director from Pawtucket. Several of his films, including *Outside Providence* and *Federal Hill*, have been set in Providence.

Matt Cottam See page 102.

Jill Craybas (1974–) is a professional tennis player who was the 1996 NCAA singles champion. She was born in Providence.

Thomas Dorr (1805–1854) was a Providence native who fought for greater voting rights for the state's residents and led Dorr's Rebellion, which resulted in Rhode Island's first constitution.

Peter Farrelly (1956–) and **Bobby Farrelly (1958–)**, natives of Cumberland, are a film writing and directing team. They have made many successful films including *Dumb and Dumber*.

John Goddard (1724–1785) of Newport was the leading cabinetmaker of his day. Today his work is extremely valuable.

Jabez Gorham (1792–1869) was a Providence silversmith who founded a company in 1842 that produced fine silver items.

Bobby (left) and Peter Farrelly

Samuel Gorton (1592–1677) was a religious leader banished from Massachusetts. He settled in Rhode Island and founded the town of Warwick.

Robert Gray (1755–1806) was a native of Tiverton who sailed around the world and explored what became the northwest United States.

Theodore Francis Green See page 64.

Nathanael Greene See page 46.

Henry Hassenfeld See page 101.

John Christian Hopkins (1960–) is a member of the Narragansett Nation who writes about Indian affairs for several newspapers and has written a book about the aftermath of King Philip's War.

Julia Ward Howe See page 81.

Alice Winsor Hunt (1872–1968) was a relative of Roger Williams noted for her social work. She led the fight to protect children in the workplace.

Anne Hutchinson See page 35.

Sissieretta Joyner Jones See page 82.

Ida Lewis See page 58.

Davey Lopes

Debra Messing

Charles I. D. Looff (1852–1918) was born in Denmark and later moved to Providence. He is remembered for the carousels he created for parks throughout the United States.

Davey Lopes (1945–) was a second baseman for the Los Angeles Dodgers for nine seasons before becoming a manager and coach in the major leagues. He was born in East Providence.

H. P. Lovecraft (1890–1937), a native of Providence, wrote strange, dark science fiction and horror stories. His work greatly influenced later writers.

David Macaulay (1946–) is a graduate of the Rhode Island School of Design in architecture. He lives in Rhode Island and writes books that explain the construction of different kinds of buildings. His works include *Cathedral* and *The Way Things Work*.

Seth MacFarlane (1973–) is a graduate of the Rhode Island School of Design and the creator of the TV cartoon *Family Guy*, which is set in Rhode Island.

Debra Messing (1968–) is a TV and film actor. She was born in New York but grew up in East Greenwich, outside of Providence.

Metacomet See page 39.

Annie Smith Peck (1850–1935) was a mountain climber and scholar. In 1908, the Providence native became the first person to climb Nevado Huascarán.

Oliver Hazard Perry (1785–1819), a native of South Kingstown, was a naval hero who commanded the U.S. fleet on the Great Lakes during the War of 1812. He led U.S. forces to a victory over the British, giving Americans control of the Great Lakes.

Elizabeth Roberts See page 89.

Allison Rogers See page 19.

Ruth J. Simmons (1945–) is the president of Brown University. The great-granddaughter of slaves, she is the first African American to serve as president of an Ivy League school.

Gilbert Stuart (1755–1828) was born in North Kingstown and went to Europe to study painting. He later painted many important figures in early American history, including George Washington.

Meredith Vieira

Thomas Tew (?–1695) was known as the Rhode Island Pirate. From his base in Newport, he sailed as far as Africa looking for treasure.

Giovanni da Verrazzano (1485?–1528) was an Italian explorer who entered Narragansett Bay in 1524. He was the first European known to visit Rhode Island.

Meredith Vieira (1953–) is a television journalist from Providence. After working for a time in her home state, she went on to appear on national TV news shows and serve as a cohost of the *Today* show.

Jemima Wilkinson (1752–1819) was the daughter of a Quaker family in Cumberland. She traveled as a preacher, spreading her religious beliefs.

Roger Williams (c. 1603–1683) was a Puritan minister who was banished from Massachusetts for his religious views. He founded Providence in 1636 and helped Rhode Island become a colony.

James Woods (1947–), who grew up in Warwick, is a film and television actor. He has starred in the TV series *Shark* and appeared in films such as *Ghosts of Mississippi*.

James Woods

RESOURCES

BOOKS

Nonfiction

Burgan, Michael. *Roger Williams: Founder of Rhode Island*. Minneapolis: Compass Point Books, 2006.

D'Agostino, Thomas. *Haunted Rhode Island*. Atglen, Pa.: Schiffer Publishing, 2006.

D'Entremont, Jeremy. *The Lighthouses of Rhode Island*. Beverly, Mass.: Commonwealth Editions, 2006.

Fisher, Leonard Everett. *To Bigotry No Sanction: The Story of the Oldest Synagogue in America*. New York: Holiday House, 1998.

Levy, Janey. *The Wampanoag of Massachusetts and Rhode Island*. New York: PowerKids Press/Rosen Publishing Group, 2005.

McDermott, Jesse. *Rhode Island, 1636–1776*. Washington, D.C.: National Geographic Society, 2006.

Fiction

Avi. *Something Upstairs: A Tale of Ghosts*. New York: Orchard Books, 1988.

Babbitt, Natalie. *Tuck Everlasting*. Santa Barbara, Calif.: ABC-CLIO, 1987.

Curtis, Alice Turner. *A Little Maid of Narragansett Bay*. Bedford, Mass.: Applewood Books, 1998.

Licameli, Doris. *Rowing to the Rescue: The Story of Ida Lewis, Famous Lighthouse Heroine*. Morrisville, N.C.: Lulu Enterprises, 2006.

Lisle, Janet Taylor. *Black Duck*. New York: Sleuth/Philomel, 2006.

DVDs

Italian Americans and Federal Hill. Seven Fishes Productions, 2006.
Mill Times. PBS Home Video, 2006.
Roger Williams and Rhode Island. Schlessinger Media, 2006.

WEB SITES AND ORGANIZATIONS

African Slave Markers in Colonial Newport
www.colonialcemetery.com/Home.htm
For more information about the slave trade in Newport and the slaves who lived and died there.

Narragansett Indian Tribe
www.narragansett-tribe.org
The official Web site of the only tribe in Rhode Island recognized by the U.S. government includes a history of the Narragansett people.

Quahog.org
www.quahog.org
A fun and informative look at Rhode Islanders and the history of their state.

Rhode Island Government Online
www.ri.gov
The official State of Rhode Island and Providence Plantations Web site has links to all branches of government.

Rhode Island Historical Preservation & Heritage Commission
www.preservation.ri.gov/survey/publications.php
This state agency has surveys of important historical sites in all 39 Rhode Island towns and a statewide survey of archaeological sites.

Roger Williams National Memorial
www.nps.gov/rowi
To learn more about the founder of Rhode Island and the memorial honoring him.

Save the Bay
www.savebay.org
For information about efforts to protect Narragansett Bay.

Slater Mill
www.slatermill.org
To learn more about Samuel Slater and the mill he built in Pawtucket.

Visit Rhode Island
www.visitrhodeisland.com
For more information on historical and cultural sites and recreation activities in Rhode Island.

INDEX

★ ★ ★

AUTHOR'S TIPS AND SOURCE NOTES

★ ★ ★

Growing up in Connecticut, I spent a great deal of time in Rhode Island, lounging on beaches, getting lost in Providence, and exploring the streets of Newport. Wherever I went, I was impressed by the history and natural beauty of the smallest state.

To research this book, I visited Rhode Island. I also read many books. Particularly helpful were *Rhode Island: A History* by Brown University historian William G. McLoughlin, and *Rhode Island: A Genial History* by local reporters Paul F. Eno and Glenn Laxton. Details on sites I didn't visit myself came from Web sites and sources such as *Off the Beaten Path: Rhode Island* by Robert Curley. For some of the lesser-known facts about the state, I turned to Ryder Windham's *You Know You're in Rhode Island When . . .* The State of Rhode Island Web sites and the *Providence Journal* site were essential for information on the state government, economy, and current affairs.